FIND YOUR
BELOVED

CREATING DELICIOUS COMPANIONSHIP

ROSINE KUSHNICK

Copyright © Rosine Kushnick, 2020

All rights reserved. No part of this publication may be reproduced, distributed, or transmitted in any form or by any means, including photocopying, recording, digital scanning, or other electronic or mechanical methods, without the prior written permission of the publisher, except in the case of brief quotations embodied in critical reviews and certain other noncommercial uses permitted by copyright law.

ISBN: 978-1-95-036728-3

Published by
Lifestyle Entrepreneurs Press
Las Vegas, NV

If you are interested in publishing through Lifestyle Entrepreneurs Press, write to: *Publishing@LifestyleEntrepreneursPress.com*

Publications or foreign rights acquisitions of our catalog books.
Learn More: *www.LifestyleEntrepreneursPress.com*

Printed in the USA

DISCLAIMER: No part of this publication may be reproduced or transmitted in any form or by any means, mechanical or electronic, including photocopying or recording, or by any information storage and retrieval system, or transmitted by email without permission in writing from the author. Neither the author nor the publisher assumes any responsibility for errors, omissions, or contrary interpretations of the subject matter herein. Any perceived slight of any individual or organization is purely unintentional. Brand and product names are trademarks or registered trademarks of their respective owners.

Cover Design: Jennifer Stimson
Editor: Cory Hott
Author Photo Courtesy of: Carl Cox

Advance Praise

"Find Your Beloved is a well-written, easy-to-read book about a groundbreaking approach to healing and creating relationships. If you are looking for a deep connection with someone, I highly recommend reading it. It is a book written from a place of deep love and it takes you on a journey to find your."
— Dr. Hector E. Garcia, Garcia Holistic Center

"*Find Your Beloved* has opened up a whole new way of life for me. A life that is filled with my inner magic, in deep connection with those I love. Paradoxically, the deeper I dove into the subject matter of relationships applying what Rosine outlines in detail in this book, the more my work as a theater director excelled. I feel totally free and deeply connected, all at once. If you want to live life at its fullest, I highly recommend this beautiful read infused with the energy of the heart."
— Marta Malinowska, theater director

"You're about to be treated to an in-depth understanding of how Mother, Amazon, Lover, and Wise Woman, the feminine aspects of the Archetypal blueprints contained within each of us are right there waiting to inform us and to be integrated as guiding sources and an opportunity to weave them into ever expanding lives of more joy, fulfillment, ease, relationship and romance. This journey can get complicated at times, but you'd be hard pressed to find a more skillful and knowledgeable expert to guide you through the mysterious forces at play in your life sprouting from the subconscious mind and collective unconsciousness of our planet."
— Albert Pellissier, founder of ManCamp.net

"The process and wisdom that Rosine shares so generously in her book *Find Your Beloved* has completely changed my life. As a result, I relate and connect with other people, in particular with men, in a totally different fashion. It has opened my mind and heart so I can build strong and meaningful relationships that are based on unconditional love, mutual respect and on truly seeing someone for who they are. I just love it and recommend anyone looking for their beloved to pick up a copy."

– Magdalena Strojna, executive business coach at Forever Living Products

"Do you secretly wish and long for better relationships, a better career, feeling more capable and competent, feeling worthy and more self-assured? The book "Find Your Beloved-Your Guide to Attract True Love" will take you on that journey. Rosine is thoughtful, kind, reassuring and deeply committed to your success and well-being. She has outlined a relationship road map for all of us that brings complex issues into the light. Find Your Beloved changes the playing field; the shadows are moving into the light and it is time we all move into the light."

– Bob O'Brien, founder of ServeAndGrow.com

Thank you, Gurumayi, for setting my heart ablaze.

Table of Contents

Foreword 1

Chapter 1: The Most Daunting and Important Thing You Will Ever Do 5

Chapter 2: The Gift of The Challenging Relationship 13

Chapter 3: A Guide to The Guide 19

Chapter 4: The Only Way Out Is Through 25

Chapter 5: Who Created Your Relationships Thus Far 43

Chapter 6: The Secret Maps 51

Chapter 7: Connection, Connection, Connection 59

Chapter 8: Move from Surviving to Thriving 81

Chapter 9: The Key to Full Self-Expression 89

Chapter 10: Turn on Your Inner GPS 105

Chapter 11: The Keys to Find Your Beloved 113

Chapter 12: Nothing Will Work Unless You Do 117

Chapter 13: To Change Your Life, You Need to Change Your Priorities 131

Acknowledgments 139

Thank You 141

About the Author 143

Foreword

The day my path crossed with Rosine Kushnick's – while attending a four-day women's retreat (a story in itself) – was a memorable one. It was a critical turning point in my own evolution toward creating a life of joyful success and meaningful connection, a deeper understanding of myself and how to relate to women, as well as bolstering my mission of leading other men toward the same outcome so that we can be there for you.

You may wonder why the foreword of this book for women is written by a man, and that is because I'm hand-delivering a message to you from the man you're looking for. I want to assure you that he is also longing patiently for you and doing his best to make his way to you as he navigates his own uncertainty, doubts, and fears. He, too, craves the deep connection, peace, and purpose that springs from the magic of a healthy, mutually respectful relationship built on a foundation of unconditional love. He, like you, is also a courageous person doing the inner work that leads to the sustained growth and the happiness you both desire that is your well-deserved birthright.

It wasn't until I met and started to work with Rosine that I realized most of my efforts would be in vain without a clear understanding of the unseen forces of my subconscious at play. She's the wisest, most knowledgeable, and gifted guide who I've ever had the privilege and good fortune to meet when it comes to this unchartered, deep, and complicated ocean of the subconscious mind and the collective unconscious forces at work. Her generosity and loving imperative to help me, my clients, and others to not only navigate, but to also integrate these mysterious forces and disowned aspects of ourselves, led to mind-blowing permanent emotional healing for myself, as well as witnessing life-changing miracles for many others.

What she's discovered here is a game changer. Rosine has found the deeply-buried hidden treasure maps and coded blueprints of the archetypal energies residing inside each of our subconscious minds. She knows they're waiting for us when we're ready to access them, and even better, how to flip the switch of permanent integration, which aligns us with their vibration and therefore gains the ability to attract what we want and desire.

There is so much going on inside of us that we are unaware of that profoundly affects us, many times hampering and thwarting our efforts to navigate successfully though life, leaving us befuddled and confused as to why. Rosine knows why, in spite of our best efforts and countless strategies, things don't turn out as we desire, as we continually repeat patterns that do not serve us.

An early life event can seem so innocent, yet the impact on your adult life can be confounding. I'll never forget the day that Rosine artfully guided me to my seven-year-old experience of Mom marrying my stepfather. He's a great guy. He took care of us kid and was nice to us. They're still married today, and approaching their fiftieth anniversary. I've never had a bad word to say about this gracious, generous, and loving guy. "But what about when you were seven?" Rosine prompted. "I don't like it, and there's nothing I can do about it!" was my answer. Instantly, I realized I'd heard this programmed script running in my head throughout my entire adult life. Whenever things didn't go my way, "there was nothing I could do about it." I'd become a wounded warrior somewhere along the way still paying the price from an unhealed festering wound in my fifties.

Her expert understanding is unparalleled when it comes to the consequences that resulted from our best efforts to survive and cope with life's trials and trauma. Most importantly, her most valuable gift to us is in her ability to help us to become more aware while implementing the quickest, most effective, efficient, and permanent path to undo the numerous episodes of splintering we've undergone and set us firmly on a new path of reintegration and wholeness. She introduced me to the concept of integrating the energy of the archetypal warrior. Then and only then was my warrior healed and instantly found I "could do something" about anything I didn't like in my life.

After working with Rosine to integrate the archetypal energies of the father, warrior, lover, and magician with my men's group, I was shocked that no one had yet written and explored these energies of connection, thriving, self-expression, and Intuition and the counterparts for women and the divine feminine. Rosine assumed the responsibility and as she states throughout this book, that we all have the need for both the feminine and masculine to be developed inside of us to be fully whole and be able to step up and embody the full force and presence of our being. She's created a roadmap to these ancestral roadmaps with this work.

You're about to be treated to an in-depth understanding of how mother, amazon, lover, and wise woman, the feminine versions of the archetypes, contained within each of us, are there waiting to inform us and be integrated as guiding sources with an opportunity to weave them into ever expanding lives of more joy, fulfillment, ease, and relationship. This journey can get complicated at times. As Rosine points out, with four archetypes each for feminine and masculine, one mature and one immature for each of those, and two shadow or unseen aspects of each version, the vulnerable and the protector, this leaves you with thirty-two potential rogue characters in your subconscious to deal with as you attempt to wrangle them back into your awareness to benefit from their gifts. No wonder things can get crazy in someone's life. Relax, however, and know that you have a trusted, trained, and highly experienced expert at the wheel of this journey to help you navigate the unchartered waters of the subconscious and the soul.

By way of these true stories within this book from Rosine's own personal experience and those of her clients, you'll come to recognize the variety of symptoms created by the cast of shadow aspects of the archetypes, how they've been playing mysterious havoc in your life, where they came from in the first place, how they interact with each other and affect the whole, and hopefully the relief that comes from finally understanding what's really happening in our complex human nature that's painting the picture of your current circumstances and ultimately learning "you can do something about it."

Albert Pellissier
Founder of ManCamp.net
Baton Rouge, Louisiana

Chapter 1

The Most Daunting and Important Thing You Will Ever Do

"A deep sense of love and belonging is an irreducible need of all people. We are biologically, cognitively, physically, and spiritually wired to love, to be loved, and to belong. When those needs are not met, we don't function as we were meant to. We break. We fall apart. We numb. We ache. We hurt others. We get sick."
— Brené Brown

The realm of relationships is possibly one of the most complex and potentially most painful arenas that you can get stuck in, especially when things go south or stay south. It can be so painful and confusing, and you can end up feeling isolated, despaired, and hopeless. It can be a most overwhelmingly agonizing, frustrating, and perplexing experience. Maybe needing to find what is wrong with you so you can finally fix it once and for all has robbed you of your self-esteem, your self-confidence — at least, whatever was left of it.

Did you pick up this book because you are still heartbroken from one or more of your last relationships and you have held onto your dream, however faint it may be, to finally have a relationship that works? Or maybe your past relationships weren't that painful and confusing; there simply haven't been any, and you are now ready for one.

The majority of relationship patterns you have inherited from generations ago are actually toxic and lead to despair, frustration, confusion, violence, and most of all, loneliness. Even though they produced relationships that are of the norm, they still are toxic. Outdated relationship patterns usually involve the necessity for one or both people to change who they are in order to beget love from the other. That does constitute toxicity over time, for sure, yet it goes by unnoticed most of the time. And we simply wonder why love doesn't feel that great.

The desire to be in a relationship is not only normal but deeply wired into who you are as human being. Belonging to someone – or rather a whole tribe – is hardwired into your biological make up. You do not desire anything that is not for you to have. You may have to make extra effort; you may have to make huge efforts to get there. But if it is a desire of your heart, then it is possible. All desires of your heart were placed there by the most benevolent force, a force that does not delight in taunting you. It only delights in you growing and reaching for more of the light you already are. If you have a desire, ever so faint, to find your beloved, this is a journey for you where you will find the most significant treasures along the way. Every journey toward a true heart's desire is paved with gifts, surprises, and revelations.

You have a beautiful and sincere heart, and maybe relationships have not yet worked out for you the way you always hoped for and dreamed of. I am really sorry about that. It can be a painful experience – an experience that leaves you wondering what point your life has if there is no love. It can be like a wet blanket, muffling all other activities you may pour much effort into. Without being able to share all of it with that special someone, it can truly lose all its meaning.

When you experience hardship in the arena of relationships, you might sometimes wonder, "What is wrong with me?" You can get so lost in trying to figure out what to do, who to be, whom to date, that often the easiest – and seemingly most sensemaking – explanation is that of concluding, there is something terribly wrong with you. And if only you knew what that was, you could just fix it. And you go on a quest to fix yourself.

I want you to know that there is nothing wrong with you. Your life simply has been a logical enfoldment of one thing after another, creating your current reality. That's all. There is truly nothing wrong with you. And whatever has been blocking the true love you so desire can be unblocked.

I do believe that as human beings we are wired to look to complete ourselves. Often spouses are referred to as "our better half." This colloquial way of referring to a spouse kind of implies that spouses become a new entity, the couple.

I find that in this day and age some people frown upon when you say that you do not feel complete or whole on your own. The notion that you are to access everything you need from only within has been misunderstood.

I agree that our inner nature is astounding, limitless, and amazing. And yet, there is nothing like sharing it with someone else and creating a whole new life, possibly even new life as in children. There is nothing like augmenting this inner amazingness, making it more colorful and resilient by combining with another.

Has anyone ever made you feel like there might something wrong with you for wanting to be with someone else, as in, "Why don't you just love yourself more?" If so, do not let that bother you. There is nothing wrong with you, and loving yourself involves removing your inner blocks to allow love from another human being to flow in.

Everything you experience in life is ultimately your own responsibility, no one else's. However, often what you create and are responsible for you are not aware of how you created it or why. You are not aware of your unconscious thoughts and feelings that are hidden away somewhere in dark corners of your psyche. And so it becomes easy to use the idea that you are responsible for everything you created in your life as a means of beating yourself up. "Why did I do that? Again. I can't believe I create this much misery for myself. See – I do suck. See – I don't deserve anything good in my life. Otherwise, why would I be creating this nonsense."

It is a fine line to walk between taking responsibility for all that you create and also not blaming yourself for what you find you created. Instead, gathering up the gusto to dissect what and why you created something so you can create something you love with awareness and precision is what we are looking for here.

I will give you a much deeper understanding and appreciation of how particular relationship dynamics came about in your life. And part of the process is such that it will fill you with compassion and understanding for yourself and your creations rather than criticism and blame. And, most importantly, it will give you access to the power to change it for good.

Do you ever wonder why is it that everyone else is in a relationship and not you? What did they do so they deserve that? What is their secret sauce? Maybe your friends are all married; maybe they have happy families, and you are still alone, not sure if you will ever find the right one.

Being in a loving relationship truly is life-giving. Not finding your beloved can be a demoralizing experience. It can feel like going in circles — self-defeating circles that can leave you high and dry, exhausted and sad, distraught and possibly even angry. You can get stuck in pain, shame, and frustration for not being able to find your beloved.

Maybe it hurts so deeply that you can't find joy in life any longer. Or worse, you may buy more and more into this creeping feeling that something is deeply and intrinsically wrong with you.

You may have tried to create that loving relationship in your life. Maybe you went for it; you trusted both yourself and your partner, and you went all-out and ended up with an unbearable pile of hurt. And with that, possibly you have concluded that this is not for you after all.

What you ask for is not much, you might tell yourself — just a decent man to love and who will love you back. How hard can it be? However, each time you reach for the stars, you end up with a handful of mud.

Maybe you found what looked like your perfect love, yet after some time, he withdrew from you, the emotional connection dwindled, and everything became stale, distant and ultimately a confusing, demoralizing mess. Maybe there was lying, violating, hiding, cheating, any combination of which makes it hard to find the resolve to open one's heart and try again. Especially if you have done that a few times without things actually changing, it starts to make no sense.

In fact, many women become ambivalent about whether or not they want to be with someone. Deep down, they absolutely want to be with someone, but closer to the surface, it tends to sound more like, "I will just focus on loving myself and my friends and family" — a guise of love, that really says, "I no longer can do this. It is too painful. I don't know how to make it go any different this time. I really can't afford any more heartbreak."

Some go as far as concluding that they do not need connection and that they like being alone. And although being alone can be delicious and most wonderful, it can also be a form of avoidance. Avoidance of transforming that which has been so painful and/or destructive previously. If you don't know how or have no reason to believe this time will be different, it makes no sense to undertake that journey. And it is normal to write the importance of relationship off. We all do it at times. We tell ourselves that we are better off alone, as it causes much less trouble.

It does seem to work to some degree; life does become more bearable when you simply deny yourself the need for connection. You have more control over circumstances that seem out of control; you can choose to be content with what you have and pretend you are reasonably happy. And no one is going to mess with that. Yet what may linger underneath the attempt to pretend you don't need anyone is a departure from who you really are and what you truly desire in life, and any such departure can cause great harm to yourself over time. It can damage your self-esteem, your sense of self; it can even damage your career as you no longer show up as all that you can be. It can also end up being damaging to the people and friendships that are in your life and even to your body. It is not a solution that works so well for you in the long run. At times, you need a reprieve, for sure, but in the long haul, if you do not follow your heart's desire, you will never find all the treasures that are waiting for you along the way.

There are, of course, scientific studies showing that being in a meaningful and secure relationship with a significant other is a direct indicator of mental, emotional, and financial wellbeing. It shows clearly that humans – women and men alike – do much better when they are in a loving and supportive relationship.

Our relationships dominate the quality of our lives and also that of our neighborhoods, communities, and nations. The quality of our individual relationships has a big influence on the foundation of world peace.

Healthy relationships promote happier immune systems, lower levels of anxiety and depression, contribute to better sleep, and give us a sense of worthiness. All in all, good relationships nurture us and make us feel better about life and ourselves.

Your heart's desire of finding your beloved is worth finding. I know you know that already. I simply want to let you know that you are right for not having given up on your dream. Being in a relationship where you can genuinely be yourself and give the other person the space to be fully who they are is a deeply fulfilling experience. Being part of each other's growth and expansion is like nothing else. Being with someone who is deeply committed to you and who only wants you to thrive, and vice versa, is the most supportive and grounding experience you can have that can catapult you like nothing else into becoming who you truly want to be in this world.

I would like to offer you a route where you no longer have to go down the rabbit hole of what is wrong with you, what is wrong with life, what is wrong with men, and turn this around.

I am here to cheer you on and root for you on this transforming journey of you opening up the doors for true love to show up. By virtue of you having picked up this book, I know you are heeding your heart's desire, and I know you can't go wrong.

By virtue of you having this desire, I also know that you deserve to find him.

I am going to share with you how you can make a happy relationship a reality for you. You deserve it; it is possible, and why not? I would like to ask you to hang in there with me, open your heart and mind, and come along.

Please make yourself a cup of tea, and keep reading. You are on the right track.

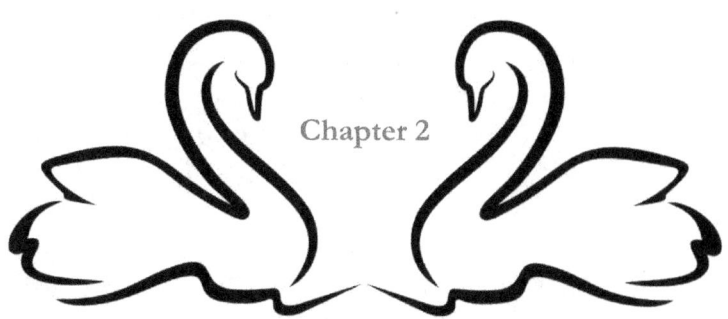

The Gift of the Challenging Relationship

"Everyone says love hurts, but that is not true. Loneliness hurts. Rejection hurts. Losing someone hurts. Envy hurts. Everyone gets these things confused with love, but in reality, love is the only thing in this world that covers up all the pain and makes someone feel wonderful again. Love is the only thing in this world that does not hurt."

– Liam Neeson

My track record of relationship looks like a series of failures, yet I used those opportunities to learn and grow in ways I could have never imagined accomplishing in any other way. You can say I milked every opportunity to the max. It is in relationship with others that we get to know more about what our personality is composed of, the good and the bad. And I wanted all of it. I wanted to see what I could only see in the relentless mirror of a relationship, what I could not see about myself on my own. We cannot transform something that we cannot see and own.

My failed relationships drove me to find a new approach with great fervor. It was not an option for me to give up nor to settle for something that doesn't work. I needed to find a solution; something that explained to me why a relationship didn't work, what my part in it was, so I could stop recreating the same heartaches.

A therapist once suggested I consider the option of never understanding what happened or what went wrong. Not me. I wanted answers, explanations, and solutions.

And, lo and behold, I discovered something quite astounding that not only gave me the answers and access to transformation I needed but also for all my clients.

When I was seven years old, I made herbal salves for my animals using an old book with herbal medicinal recipes. One of my uncles even volunteered to drink my concoction to allegedly lower his blood pressure made of white wine with woodruff steeped in it. Why not?

In my early teen years, I taught myself how to read tarot cards and started a meditation practice, taught by my aunt who liked spending time in a Buddhist monastery in Japan. My meditation practice has since changed; nevertheless, it almost adds up to forty-some years of meditation. I studied all kinds of healing methods, some more geared to support the physiology (homeopathy and herbalism), some geared to bring about change through working with the mind and the energy of things (reiki, innergetics, matrix energetics, reading the akashic records), others yet geared to resolve deep seated emotional trauma.

At some point in my life, I lost my ability to speak, and the doctors kindly let me know that if I was lucky, I would be able to communicate with a whisper but most likely that would go as well over time. That was not exactly a plan I subscribed to, and I set out to find a different outcome. I did. A few years later, I got my ability to speak back, and along with that, I acquired quite a few healing abilities that I learned from various teachers on my journey; some modalities were ancient, some brand new. I learned not to take anything for granted. I learned the immeasurable value of deep listening, and I learned that not giving up always rewards us with something precious.

Throughout it all, I learned to trust and develop my intuitive abilities, which is one of the gifts I use in all my work; I have a laser beam x-ray vision which allows me to save my clients enormous amount of time by cutting right to the chase.

I grew up with a mother who at the time was considered by other children and mothers as "very strict and stern." Nowadays in the U.S.A., her approach to child rearing would be labeled as severe emotional, mental, and physical child abuse. Pain breeds pain. Hurt people hurt people. She was raised in an environment where emotional needs were not understood, not appreciated, and not tended to. Emotional neglect and abuse are the natural expressions of that, which can scar anyone for life. Needless to say that this has been handed down for generations. My mother in particular coped with her abuse in a way that some would consider severely abusive – an environment where I had to dodge daily explosive eruptions of the nastiest kind over nothing.

This taught me much. I developed an uncanny ability to read other's emotions, anticipate their moves and motives, and most of all, I learned how to be invisible and small. The more invisible I was, the safer I was. There was no way I was being heard or seen for who I was, what I needed, what my emotions were. Hence, when I moved to the U.S.A., I had no idea who I was. I hurt beyond comprehension, yet the pain was so deeply stuffed away that I had no idea it was even there. Naturally, I was confused about what I wanted and who I was. I was living in a shell of coping mechanisms that had kept me alive.

When you now add an intimate relationship to that concoction, you can only imagine how that went – not well. And guess what is a more effective way to connect with these layers of hurt, confusion, anger, despair, and so on? A relationship.

My search for something that worked, for something that delivered solutions, for something that finally made sense to me, came about in serendipitous ways; pieces fell into place when I least expected them – a sign that gave me confidence and inspired me to trust the process and keep moving forward. The further I went, the more magical it got.

One cold winter day, I was at home, ready to work, when the power went out. The work I carved out for myself that day was all going to require the usage of my computer. Since I could no longer do that, all of a sudden, I had all this time on my hands. And this brilliant idea came to mind: I could read one of my books. You see, I love books, and I don't really like reading. I have a bookshelf full of awesome, unread books. I know, it is ironic, as I am writing a book myself.

I went to my bookshelf and pulled out a book called *King, Warrior, Magician, Lover: Rediscovering the archetypes of the Mature Masculine* by Robert Moore and Douglas Gillette. I sat on my sofa and read. As I turned the pages, I got inspired to use this information in conjunction with the work I already did that had everything to do with integrating emotional trauma.

I started experimenting right away and learned at a rapid pace. Luckily, I had clients who were open to my ideas and trusted me and came along on the ride with me. The results were remarkable. It opened up a whole new possibility of bringing about different dynamics in the realm of relationships; replacing the old, dysfunctional ones with light-filled, live-giving ones.

Soon thereafter, I found myself in front of a group of about ten men who were eager to learn more about themselves and access more of their divine masculine energies. The group leader was a trusted client of mine with whom I test-drove some of this material, and he was excited to have me work with his group of men – not the most easy audience for a vulnerable experiment, but hey, I went for it.

Much happened on that day, but the most significant part for me was that I had the opportunity to work with a man, who unbeknownst to me, was told by his wife the day before that she wanted to file for divorce. They had a newborn baby in addition to a few older children. A divorce was just not a great outlook for all involved.

I dove right in and assisted him with the process that I will share with you later on for about one hour. A deep shift took place that immediately changed his inner workings in regard to connecting and relating to a significant other. He had been unconsciously running from any and all forms of intimacy. He quite literally was unable to connect deeply. That of course takes its toll on a marriage, no matter how much you try to make it work and no matter how awesome of a guy you are. If that setting is off, you simply cannot do an intimate relationship.

Within that one hour, we were able to change that setting, and he went to call his wife to tell her all about it. There were tears of love and relief, there was no longer a need for a divorce, and they are still married to this day. What was resolved on a deep, unconscious level, was his phobia that he had carried around with him all his life of connecting with a significant other, something he had no access to and no understanding of.

A series of this type of experiences like this drove me further and further into exploring the potential of this approach. What if there is a simple way, a directed and predictable way, of adjusting the inner settings on what looks like the inability to connect deeply or the tendency to destroy connection?

Naturally, I came across so much more than that, which I will go into further detail in this book, but this is how it all started: a deep wish and desire, to reset the settings that causes people to choose disconnection over connection. It became evident to me that these are settings we have no conscious access to, and most of our settings are set on "disconnect," not on "connect." Yet, as a human species, we are wired to connect. It is my deep desire to bridge the gap between what we are truly wired for and our unconscious settings so that we can live in deep connection with one another.

It is my deep wish to help repair and restore the sacred web that connects all of humanity and share my discoveries with you.

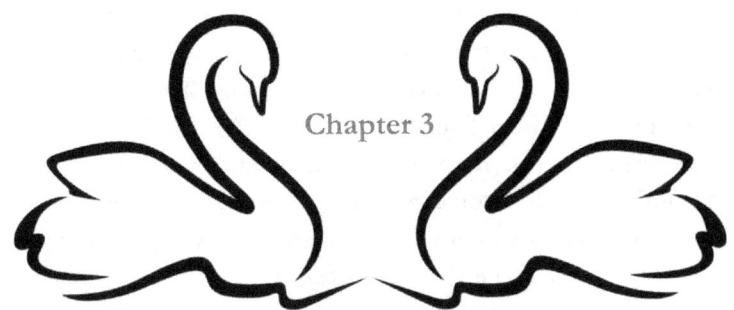

Chapter 3

A Guide to the Guide

"The minute I heard my first love story, I started looking for you, not knowing how blind that was. Lovers don't finally meet somewhere. They're in each other all along."

— Rumi

I will take you on a journey that may, on one hand, seem abstract and irrelevant, yet it has everything to do with you and how your relationships have been playing out for you this far. I encourage you to read with an open mind and heart and consider as you leaf through this book that this may contain the key to you putting the experience of accidentally repeating the same thing over and over to rest.

There is a method to this madness; I promise you.

I will share with you the components of how you can laser right into the bullseye of what caused you to choose lovers with whom you could not build a nurturing relationship.

I will share with you how I use emotional trauma resolution combined with the notion of archetypal energies of the divine feminine and masculine in a combo to patterns that prevent us from deep connection and true love.

Diving into this material and allowing yourself to do the inner work necessary to change the enfoldments of your reality is one of the best ways you can practice self-love. There is nothing more loving to yourself than to transform that which causes you deep pain. There is nothing ickier than knowing that you are responsible for what you experience, yet what you see happening in your life seems so out of control and certainly not what you asked for. What is the missing piece? Why would you possibly create a mess for yourself when clearly that is not what you want?

I will guide you through the discoveries I have made so you too can have access to this information and transform what is no longer working for you.

The information I share with you is not the only tool you will want to know about relationships. Relationships are a vast and complex matter, and they certainly benefit from us learning many different types of skills and approaches to optimize them.

You will learn all about the underlying structure, the underpinning blueprint for how relationships show up for you, which is deeply buried inside of you. You will learn how to change this blueprint, so you won't have to repeat the same annoying, frustrating, or disempowering nightmare of a relationship again.

The blueprint, if you want to call it that, is buried in the subconscious. You need an efficient way of getting there, a laser beam. You don't want to get lost in the vast ocean of the subconscious. You want to get right to the relevant switches, not sift through oodles of confusing layers of information that may or may not have anything to do with relationships. Let's get right to it. You need a direct route to where that thing that creates and informs our relationships is so we can re-wire it once and for all.

It is quite exciting, as this particular approach has not only paved the way for people to find their beloved, but also it has been a key for people to keep true love and grow it. Some have even grown babies as a result of this work.

At first, of course, it looks like the guy is the issue. And granted, when your emotional body vibrates with pain and hurt, you most likely will attract a guy who is good at pain and hurt. So there is truth to the fact that he may be the issue. However, he certainly is not the only issue in the picture. The issues buried in you will move more and more to the surface and become available for transformation. And they only become available for transformation once they are at the surface.

In this way, I have gained lots of experience in navigating the terrain of difficult and painful relationships. And I know that unfortunately this is a common and widespread malady. It can literally make us sick.

Because relationships are so central to our lives – they are part of our biological makeup – I want to share this information and assist others in making the lasting and profound change I was able to bring about in my clients and myself.

Because of the law of attraction, you tend to bring into your life exactly what is a vibrational match to your deepest reality whether you like it or not and whether you are aware of it or not. If you grew up in a dysfunctional family, as most of us have, you hold a vibration that is encoded with exactly that dysfunctional information.

Not that you have a choice, but the law of attraction brings a mate into your life that is the perfect mirror and catalyst for these unconscious patterns to come to the surface. It is like draw-salve. Whatever has not been resolved in the past will be activated and triggered.

It is an ingenious design, albeit thoroughly annoying. Let's say you have survived the childhood from hell and finally get to create your own relationship and start a family; before you know it, all that same stuff is up in your face again, and it will stay there until you have found a way to resolve and dissolve it.

The law of attraction is actually a really useful tool, as it will show you exactly what is deeply buried in you. Whatever you have attracted into your life, you are in deep resonance with it, whether you want to or not.

Whatever we experience in childhood, we encode for as normal. And if it was not for the law of attraction mirroring back weird or painful situations, we could never decode what is deeply stored within us.

Without the law of attraction mirroring back to you what is buried deep within, you would not be able to identify what is otherwise unseen to you, such as beliefs and concepts of what you are capable of.

A challenging relationship then becomes a gift – a gift to find the hidden pain and the hidden, festering wounds that keep you small and ineffective. It never means that a challenging relationship ought to remain a challenging relationship, and it certainly never means that putting up with any form of abuse is useful or beneficial; not at all. But a challenging relationship can become a powerful and effective guide into the depth of your own interiors that so badly need to come to the light.

Those relationships bear a gift of deep healing, an invitation to revisit the most painful and hidden memories if you are willing to do the work. Bringing them to the light in one way or another is the only way they will stop having a grip on you. And if you do want to create the relationship where you truly thrive, you do have to get out of those grips first.

What we will uncover in this book together is a helpful tool to go into your relationship software and reconfigure a few things so new and different relationship dynamics become second nature to you.

You will learn about the correlation of your emotional well-being and the quality of your relationships. You will also explore, how the archetypal energies, innate energies that govern our human experience, play an undeniable role in the enjoyability of your relationships.

Chapter 4

The Only Way Out Is Through

"The negative people who trigger us to feel negative emotions are messengers. They are messengers for the unhealed parts of our being."

– Teal Swan

As a human race, we are astoundingly proficient in so many areas of life; we can transplant organs. We can do brain surgery. We even know how to visit other planets. However, in the arena of emotions, I dare say, I find we operate as if we still lived somewhere in the dark ages. I think we have yet to understand how our emotional bodies really work, what they need for optimal functioning, and how to repair and maintain them.

The issue or at least one of the many issues with that is all of our relationships are an expression and reflection of our emotional wellness. In other words, our relationships can only be as well as our emotional bodies are. And if we are not yet all that competent on how to take care of emotional needs, how would we possibly do well in the arena of relationships?

Emotions are often dealt with using outdated approaches such as suppressing, overriding, controlling, or rationalizing them. People talk about having to overcome their negative emotions, which really, when you follow the thread, you will find is most often a matter of suppressing them. What these approaches can eventually lead to is a sense of being overwhelmed, depressed, anxious, or addicted to a substance or an activity. It can lead to having outbursts of anger and rage possibly accompanied by violent or abusive behaviors. It can even lead to physical disease.

Granted, any of these approaches are more useful than causing harm to oneself or others due to unbridled emotions; that is for sure. But in the long run, I am not so certain that these approaches are sustainable and that they bring the depth of connection and peace that most of us would enjoy. Emotions are a raw form of energy that run through our bodies. When we fight them or try to cage them, the energy has no way of dissipating and it will keep haunting us until they are freed.

I find it rare that a person has a truly gentle, loving, and embracing relationship with their emotions. I find that people who have done a lot of emotional integration work versus controlling/rationalizing/suppressing feel soft and supple. There is fluidity in their ways of being that puts people around them at ease. It can feel like a complex dance around an energy that is unwelcomed, and although we have all become good at this dance, there still is this humongous pink elephant in the room.

I sometimes get the impression that people relate to emotions as a nuisance, something that is in the way, something to battle and conquer.

They are guarded against their own emotions rearing their ugly head in the wrong moment, and they certainly dread the same thing happening in the people around them. Sometimes it even comes across as a sense of superiority, looking down on the person who has "emotional issues" as being less evolved.

What if allowing yourself to feel your emotions is allowing you to evolve faster?

Many people behave if there is something inherently and terribly wrong with having emotions. How could there be something wrong with having emotions if the emotional body is such a big part of the human design? All the great art that we cherish – music, dance and theater – would not exist if it was not for emotion, energy-in-motion. It is like considering our bones, nerve tissue, or any organ as something wrong and faulty in our design. Emotions are as much part of the human experience as are bones, nerve tissue, and organs, so why not embrace them and take good care of them?

I often hear judgment of emotions, as in how dumb someone is for still feeling this way or as in how ridiculous this person behaved feeling that way or how dramatic they are or how weak this person is or how pathetic someone is, how immature. I hear a lot of judgment all around, as if ultimately emotions were something dirty or an indication of one's inadequacies.

I am not promoting a display of unprocessed emotions, especially not the kind directed at someone else in a harmful way.

Everyone wants to experience happiness, fulfillment, and joy. Aren't these emotions, too? We want one end of the spectrum, but we loathe the other, and truth be told, we can only have one with the other.

So we have a few choices:

1. We can either suppress some of them or try to get rid of them. By doing so, we lose access to all of them, and we live a rather flat life, kind of a black and white version of life.
2. We can be in the throes of all of our emotions, ups and downs, a very tiring and stressful experience indeed.
3. We can learn to be with, embrace, accept, and integrate all of our emotions and live a life that is meaningful,

flowing, and delightful. Clearly, there is no right or wrong choice. It is all simply a question of what quality of life we desire and what effort we are willing or able to make.

I think that if we, as the human race, could become a little more accepting and embracing of our own and other people's emotions and not have such aversions against them, world peace would become a much higher probability.

Nora asked me for my support because her marriage was painful for her, yet she really wanted to make it work.

Nora did not know how to twist or turn to make herself feel good. She blamed herself, she blamed her husband, and all in all, it was not heading in a good direction. Day to day life was informed by keeping up a façade that things were okay, yet it was all tiring because they were not okay at all. Sadness, anger, disappointment, and annoyance had to be kept under wraps all day long. There seemed to be no wiggle room at all that would allow for change. Nora felt hopeless, defeated, and also like she failed not only her husband but also her son.

I assisted Nora in uncovering that she was raised believing that having any emotional needs was bad, and when she dug deeper, she saw that she felt shame about having emotions. She also uncovered that the way she was raised taught her that men can have their way with her, sexually and in any other way, as her mother did not protect her from her father's intrusions.

Nora identified with having to be nice, not having any needs, accommodating everyone else's needs, and feeling afraid of men. Naturally, that is a ticket for a disastrous marriage, no matter who the partner is. I was committed to supporting Nora as she resolved her side of things so deeply so she could feel again what was really true for her and what she really wanted and needed.

Nora's big accomplishment was to reconnect with her true needs and emotions without the shame and guilt for having them. I helped her to find a compassionate way to relate to her fear of men, which allowed her to find empowering ways of setting boundaries with her husband that made her feel safe and connected at the same time. She learned how to share herself with her husband and communicate with him so she could create an atmosphere of mutual understanding and trust.

The marriage changed, and her husband noticed her vulnerabilities and tended to her with more care and love. He also felt safer in sharing his emotions and needs. They grew closer and are now on a trajectory of building true in-to-me-see, also known as intimacy.

Once you move into a conscious, loving relationship with your own emotions and you stop pushing them away, judging and dreading them, you can start to create a new life. You can create new realities that nurture all of humanity. For as long as you are unconscious of your emotions or feeling an aversion toward them, you cannot transform them and reap the gifts they deliver each and every time.

I would like to share some examples of how our own relationship with emotions can affect children and perpetuate a vicious circle of creating emotional wounds that then block so many experiences later in life.

If you think of a four-year-old who is really sad about his favorite toy that just broke and who is belittled for being sad and reprimanded for not being grateful for all the other toys he has – what do you suppose he makes of that experience? Do you think he will say to himself, "Well, that is too bad the adult in my life (possibly his mom) is currently not available to empathize with my feelings of sadness because she is too busy cooking dinner, tidying up the home, and trying to keep it together even though she just got fired from her job?"

Probably not. More likely he will conclude that there is something wrong with him, because in his perception his mom is rejecting him. As a child, when our emotional experience is not validated, we experience it as a rejection. Between the age of zero and eight years old, humans are living in an emotional experience and do not have the ability yet to use a rational approach to understand what goes on around them.

Therefore, this is not just a simple rejection but rather a rejection of his entire existence. This is his experience. I am being rejected because I am sad. My mom does not like or love me when I am sad. He does not see a difference between who he is and his feelings. Every time a child has an emotional experience that is disapproved of, he or she concludes there is something wrong with him or her. Can you imagine the accumulative effect of that? And how often are the emotional expressions of a person between zero and eight years old ignored, overlooked, or simply missed? A lot.

How many times per day do you suppose a child has the experience that the adult caretaker, whether that is a parent or anyone else, does not see or validate their emotional experience? In most cases, sadly, multiple times per day.

Once a child grows older and the ability to utilize the rational mind starts to kick in around age eight, the groove of feeling unappreciated, unseen, not understood, rejected, et cetera is quite deep. It is the go-to assumption that has become as normal as getting wet in the rain. My feelings don't count for much; hence, I don't either. Naturally, that is not a conscious thought or conclusion and therefore goes un-detected for however long; it is not held up as a mirror. That mirror can look like a relationship later on, where the other person doesn't seem to not care.

If, let's say, you do grow up in an environment where only some emotions are welcomed, what are you going to do with the rest of them? Possibly shove them under the rug? Or possibly move them out into the garden shed or into the underground garage? That would make sense. When you are not seen in your emotional distress as a child, it is actually way less painful to push these emotions away than to feel the rejection or the sense of being unwanted, shamed, or criticized for having them.

You develop superpowers, superpowers that are designed to keep your emotions in check. Depending on the family and cultural environment you grew up in, you were given different, silent clues as to which emotions are more acceptable than others. One strategy is to take an emotion that seems less acceptable, shove it down, and hide it under another layer of emotion. The top layer emotion can then be one that is more culturally accepted.

For example, a little girl who has natural leadership skills and seems to boss her siblings around, raising her voice, getting assertive and pushy, might quickly be shamed into feeling bad for having these innate leadership gifts. She is told that little girls are nice, don't raise their voice, and most certainly don't boss around their older brother and his pals. Before you know it, you may have a little girl who has constructed a well-designed guise of shyness. It is much easier to pack all of these conflicting feelings of shame, resentment for being shamed, and the sheer joy of showing up bossy under a blanket of shyness than to be shamed for it.

Another example is that of complete and utter hopelessness. Feeling hopeless all the time does not have a high survival probability. Instead of feeling hopeless, we hang on to anger, a cover emotion. The anger seems to have some sort of force to it that allows us to plow forward. Or we hang on to hatred that covers up severe pain. Once you look at angry people as people who cover up their feelings of hopelessness, the picture changes quickly. Or if you look at someone who acts out on hatred and you consider that they are in excruciating pain, the fact that he/she took this action can possibly start to make sense.

It does get quite complicated and complex; that is for sure. There is nothing simple about emotions once they are forced to go underground. Nothing is what it seems, and when you go digging long enough, you usually find nothing but pain underneath any and all things that you find inconvenient about yourself or another person. There is indeed a lot of pain stored in the basement, the garden shed, the closet, wherever you managed to stuff it away into. As a child, it generally is not safe to feel the pain. Empathy is not always the first go-to by the caretakers, and what is worse than feeling pain and not being met there? Pushing it away makes much sense.

The chances of being accepted, loved, and approved of are much higher when the emotions that your caregivers, teachers and so on disapprove of are made to go away. As a result of biological wiring that always promotes survival over anything else, a child will do anything to keep the approval and/or love of his caregivers, which explains why children adapt to any and all abusive behaviors and log them in their own minds as normal.

Have you ever watched a three-year-old get upset about something? If so, you probably watched this upset evaporate before your eyes in no time. All a feeling ever wants is to be felt. And once you allow it to be felt, it does evaporate quite quickly. I find it fascinating that the original energy of an emotion actually moves swiftly and has no ill effects if allowed to just move through. However, once you get into the habit of blocking that flow, which I think there is not one exception, then it becomes the most complex, complicated, and possibly destructive event.

Not only are emotions readily willing to just move through and evaporate, they also always come with a gift. When you embrace an emotion, you receive a gift. It can be a gift of insight, wisdom, joy, relief, most often, an emotion that is simply allowed and not judged that leaves you with a feeling of peace and calm.

If you were raised in an environment where some and not all feelings were validated and empathized with, you lost the art of feeling your feelings. You have instead adapted to the art of suppressing and ignoring your feelings, as has been modeled for you and demanded of you. You inadvertently built up a reservoir, and the sheer enormity of the stored and unprocessed emotions in there, is absolutely frightening.

Over time, that causes even more reason not feel them because you know that if you open the door and you feel some of them, they all will want to be felt – quite literally an overwhelming sensation that most adults avoid having with all their might. And I don't blame them. Once the reservoir is full, it becomes quite the task to release the pressure. It is almost like having to take a teaspoon and slowly take out water, one spoon at a time, until it feels safe to use a bucket and then possibly a hose before you open the floodgate.

It can be an overwhelming endeavor and quite literally feel like it might drown you. It is often way more practical to keep the reservoir full and keep going until something breaks, an uncomfortable way to live to say the least.

If our relationships are in direct correlation with our emotional wellbeing, we can only imagine what it would be like if two people in a relationship had a huge reservoir of unprocessed emotions. Possibly disastrous? There is always the option of "managing oneself" and "pretending," which requires remaining predominantly on the surface and does allow for a decent relationship; that is true. However, the depth of connection and fulfillment is not to be had in an environment of managing and pretending. It requires so much energy to manage, plus it feels forced, fake, and like hard work – no fun at all.

As overwhelming as this may sound, I want you to know that there is a direct route to resolving key events that form the relationship dynamics.

As irrational as emotions are, there is a reason for each and every single emotion. And yes, it would be strange if emotions were rational; they are not supposed to be. When you unwind some of the emotional layers, you understand that in fact there is logic to the entire emotional jumble. The emotional jumble is totally logical. One thing led to the next, to the next, to the next. And if you take your time and go gently, your inner being will show you the way on how to untangle each and every layer. But you have to be gentle, have no demands, not push anything. Otherwise, the emotional body will not participate; it has already had enough of being pushed around.

Let's go back to the little girl who most would call bossy. I like to say she was born to lead. Let's say there was a particular moment in time where she wrestled one of her older brother's friends in the school yard and ended up on top of him with a grin. She had so much fun. She felt strong and confident, and most of all, she just thought it was so much fun that she managed to get on top of a boy who was three years older than her. She had nothing malicious in mind. She was not mean; she did not hurt the guy; she was just good at wrestling. The teacher who walked by did not think it was funny at all and immediately went into shaming mode. How dare you, who do you think you are, girls don't do that, you should be ashamed of yourself, et cetera came out of his mouth all at once. The girl went from feeling so much fun and freedom to feeling terribly bad about who she was in a split second. She did not get a message that her actions were not appreciated but rather that there was something wrong about who she was.

Shame is the most terrible emotion to feel; we literally do anything to not feel it. We run, we drink, we become addicted to whatever suits us most; in short, we find a reliable method of distraction. No one wants to feel shame. And the more shame we felt as children, the less detectable the cover-up mode is, so much so that we don't even know any longer that we feel ashamed for who we are.

As a child, we need to find a way to make that shame go away pronto. The most efficient way to make shame go away is to disown whatever brought about the shame. In the case of this little girl, it was her boisterous, fun-loving, and daring aspect, for example. We simply send that aspect of ourselves away. In reality, anything belonging to us will never go away. It will simply go into the unconscious. To the conscious mind, that is the same thing as a way because you can now no longer find it; hence, it seems it no longer exist. The scary reality is that it continues to exist, only now out of your conscious reach. It most certainly does not die and continues a life you have no control over and no idea it even exists. That is one huge component of the ninety-five percent we call unconscious. That is an efficient way as a child to make the things that make us unloved and unwanted go away. This ensures our safety and survival, which always reigns supreme. The sad part is that there are huge consequences of having made that move. The move is reversible but not without paying a price. Also, your relationships may start to make more sense to you when you consider them having been designed by aspects that are completely rogue, meaning when parts of you split off and you don't any longer know what they are and what they need, they may inadvertently make choices in your relationship domain that is not in your best interest.

In this case, feeling self-expressed, confident, funny, powerful, self-asserted, and so on was sent in a hand basket to a location in the unconscious. I like to think of the unconscious as a vast universe with endless nooks and crannies, gardens, woods, houses, spaces under the floorboards, closets, galaxies, boxes, anthills, equipped with millions of hiding places. Once you command our own gifts, abilities, and feelings to go away, they do go away.

One of the consequences is that you may wake up twenty, thirty, forty or more years later and feel that you are rather empty, jaded, confused, and possibly depressed and/or anxiety-ridden. And do you suppose in that reality is space for a great, life-giving, flourishing, and thriving relationship? Probably not so much.

Emotion is energy-in-motion. It has a simple agenda. It wants to be felt from beginning to end, not just halfway through. Whenever it is felt, it moves on. Simple enough when you are a child. But not so simple when the feeling of it is too overwhelming and unsupported.

In this case, the girl who was born to lead was not able to feel the shame, as it was too overwhelming and excruciating. Without loving, non-judgmental support from someone she could trust, she had to cut the experience of feeling this shame off. And whenever a human child cannot be present with the full emotion that wants to move through its body, the child has to create a split. The unresolved and hurt aspect becomes one part of the split, and a newly formed part whose job it is now to protect the unresolved and hurt part is created. Thus, we now have two aspects instead of one. And it is no longer an integrated part of the girl, as it had been split off, which means we now have two rogue parts of the girl's personality that are no longer within her conscious domain. Every time there is an emotional experience that the girl cannot fully experience, there is another split and another and another and another, and life starts to become more and more complex.

The vulnerable and the protector aspects create a pair, an inseparable pair that now operates within the unseen world of her unconscious. Yes, that is dangerous in more ways than one, yet it is absolutely inevitable and a most integral part of the human experience. If you are a parent reading this, don't worry. It is unavoidable; unless and until every human child is being cared for by responsible, emotionally well-integrated adults in an uninterrupted, loving, caring way, these splits will happen.

They can happen when baby number two comes home; they can happen at the birthday party where the bigger sister got all the gifts and the little boy got nothing (wasn't his birthday); they can happen when a boy is being shamed for having vulnerable emotional needs, and he is called out a sissy; they can happen when a baby is not wanted by its parents while in the womb; they can happen during an accident where no one is paying attention to the little guy. The list of what situations can cause a split if not tended to with utmost care and love is literally endless. And what you see all around you and I am sorry to say most likely within you is a compilation of enormous amounts of such splits that we are desperately trying to compensate for. In fact, every split in and of itself has its own coping mechanism.

The two aspects that form the vulnerable one and the protector one are considered shadow aspects. I find that the term "shadow" can be somewhat misleading, as it insinuates that there is something dark or bad about it when really all it means is that it is in the shadow, as in it is not in the light of our own awareness. Shadows are not necessarily bad. Shadows can be destructive, but they can also be creative and productive. The operative word is shadow, meaning it is out of our conscious awareness and control.

With each split, you lose an important part of yourself. And for those of us who seek to become whole, to live in our full potential, regaining these parts is imperative.

Let's say you feel at a loss of how to navigate your career. Who knows? There possibly had been a split where your ingenuity and resourcefulness went out the window, as had been the case of one of my clients. The moment he successfully reintegrated that part of him that was ridiculed in school (long story), he regained his quite nifty resourcefulness and ingenuity and figured out his career in no time. He literally moved himself out of debt in a brief period of time and pursued a successful career doing what he loves to do.

Or let's say you feel timid and shy when it comes to meeting new people. Likely there was a moment in time where you lost your innate curiosity to meet new people and your desire to connect. There is always a total sense-making story behind every so-called inexplicable occurrence.

Or maybe you are petrified of public speaking. Possibly you had to stuff the part of you that just loves to entertain others, tell stories and jokes, far away as you were ridiculed or made wrong for it in one way or another.

And maybe you are just feeling severe anxiety, are confused, and have a really hard time getting out of bed in the morning. Most likely, you lost a whole bunch of parts, and they are waiting for you to reconnect with them.

A process of rational recollection of said events will not resolve the split. I have observed many people who are aware of their blocks, aware of their suppressed emotions, aware of the fact that the emotion stems from an event that took place a long time ago, and rather than going into the situation through the perspective of the child, they go at it as the adult. There is a sense of coercion and pushing an agenda that yet again will not work for that child aspect. It never did work, and it never will work; until and unless you are willing to meet the child in its own reality – which, granted, is a limited one – you cannot pry it out of its confinement.

Taking this approach will not undo the damage, and it will not reintegrate the lost parts. In order for the parts and emotions to be fully reintegrated, the emotion related to the experience needs to be felt and experienced. That is the part that most people find really inconvenient because, again, feeling emotions, especially emotions that are considered negative emotions, such as hopelessness, powerlessness, hatred, anger, fear and so on, is not popular. What caused the split in the first place was the inability of the child to feel the full experience of the emotion. The energy-in-motion got stuck. It is kind of logical that the energy would get stuck if the child was in a situation where it was not understood and supported. That is usually exactly the element that was missing. In order to fully reintegrate it, a safe space has to be held for the adult to allow that inner child (and there are many of them, as many as there are splits) to now experience and thus release the emotional energy. Once the emotional energy is released, it is done. It will not linger; it will not rear its ugly head; it no longer creates any pressure; it is gone. That is one of the main reasons, other than regaining one's own gifts, that I find that deep integration work to be way more sustainable than simply using the mind to choosing new thoughts.

I have witnessed the most amazing transformations when an old stuck, icky emotion that the person wasn't even aware of clogged up their life is given the safety and validation it needed all along. It is so extremely simple to resolve the deepest emotional wounds. It may not be easy to do, but it is simple. And if it is not simple, I suggest that maybe it is not the emotional body getting the long sought-after relief, but rather the mind is getting some exercise, doing what it loves to do, analyzing, trying to comprehend, categorizing, and so on.

I think one way in which we get tripped up in our emotional integration is that we learn that having certain emotions is bad. This varies from culture to culture, but in general, there certainly is a stigma on some and not on others.

We have a deep resistance to feeling anger or hatred because by just feeling it we do something we have been told all of our lives is wrong. The key here is, that we simply have to feel the emotion. We do not have to act on it. In fact, it is not advisable to act on the so-called negative emotions. Acting on them always creates disconnect – always. And it is the web of connectedness that we put in so much effort to restoring. Acting on those emotions would be counterproductive; hurling anger at someone damages our connection with that person.

That does not mean, however, you should not feel these emotions. There is a huge difference between ignoring/suppressing, feeling, and acting on emotion. An emotion is an energy current that is felt in the physical body. Feeling that current means you are feeling the emotion.

Often clients ask me: What does it mean to feel the emotion and not act on it? You can literally sit on your couch and feel the anger and not act on it, and it will change all by itself as long as you don't wish for it to go away, judge it, or make yourself wrong for feeling it. Then take note of what the anger delivered to you – most likely a message about something you put up with and that you need to address. Once the anger has dissipated, you can address the need in an amicable way.

A few thoughts on physical symptoms. I do believe that the first layer of any kind of disturbance is created on an emotional level. It can easily be as early as at conception and/or in utero. When there is any kind of emotional stress on the mother's side, in her environment, her relationships, it can affect the baby tremendously and influence the development of its physiology.

In particular, this may occur when the mother was either unaware of being pregnant and hence did not notice the baby or, worse, was aware and did not want the baby. Naturally, there are understandable circumstances and reasons for a woman not to want a pregnancy. No doubt. However, what those emotions and energies do for the embryo/fetus are quite devastating.

These are patterns that form, that become part of the root of our emotional pain, and so when you can go into womb and birth trauma and release some or all of the stored emotional contortions, it has an incredible effect on our present age self. Regardless of where exactly on the spectrum of zero to eight years old a trauma takes place, the trauma can lodge itself so deeply into the subconscious that the only way of communicating with you is through the means of a physical pain or disease.

When you relate to any and all physical imbalance as a means of a part of you that has been long buried, to get your attention, you embark on a magical journey. What seemed like the ultimate impediment to your well-being (let's say a serious disease) can now become the most amazing harbinger.

The pain/disease can alert you to what you had to disown such a long time ago; you literally have no recollection, no access via your conscious mind. Also, mind you, some of the greatest traumatic impacts can come about through seemingly mundane events that neither you nor anyone around you would have marked as a marking experience.

For that reason, I treasure any and all physical challenges I may have and tend to them as precious leads to hidden treasures. Any trauma that gets released is indeed a treasure box. And with the integration of the unprocessed emotion, the treasures are delivered in their full glory.

The majority of what I have learned on how to restore the emotional body to its suppleness I have received from Teal Swan; she has seen it all and went through it all when it comes to emotional trauma and developed and incredibly wise and compassionate approach on resolving it. I have great respect and admiration for her, for everything she went through, and for what she chose to make out of it. Talk about making lemonade out of the lemons life hands you.

Chapter 5

Who Created Your Relationships Thus Far

"Love is not an emotion; it is your existence."

– Rumi

Bottom line, what has been missing for you is true connection and intimacy. I like to think of intimacy not as a definition that sex is part of a relationship but rather intimacy as in having to do with truly seeing one another, understanding one another, and connecting deeply, connecting not just on mental, emotional, and physical level but truly being able to enjoy the phenomenon that we are indeed connected by virtue of all being made out of the same substance – called love – and simply being present to love that already is.

Some like to describe intimacy as in "in-to-me-see." It is a state where you allow someone else to truly see you, including all your insecurities, fears of inadequacy, your worries that if you were truly seen, then they surely would leave you or control you or use you. "In-to-me-see" is a state you experience when you can put these concerns aside and allow yourself to be seen deeply and also see into the other without judgment, conditions, or agendas.

When you think about finding your beloved, you think about someone with whom you can truly be yourself, someone who does not focus on your flaws but rather sees your beauty, your strength, your gifts and talents. You think of someone who will love you unconditionally for who you are and allow you to become more and more of who you want to be in this world, making the finest contribution you are here to make. And most likely, within this wish is also a deep desire to give your love to someone and to support him, giving him the space to be who he truly is.

What I observe in all the women I have worked with is that at the end of the day what matters most to them is emotional intimacy. Sexual intimacy generally does not mean as much when it is not in conjunction with the emotional intimacy; the sexual connection and desire usually dwindles when the emotional intimacy does. And the opposite is true as well for a woman; when the emotional intimacy can be restored, it usually brings back the sexual intimacy as well.

For that reason, I encourage the women I work with to focus first on building true emotional intimacy before venturing into the sexual aspect of the relationship. Most women have this undefined hope that somehow by having sex the emotional intimacy that they crave to have with their significant other will come about all by itself, when really that is not a way to build emotional intimacy. Sexual encounters create profound emotional ties but not necessarily emotional intimacy. It is these ties that get in the way of a woman being able to see a man for who he is without getting all blurry-eyed. It also makes it a lot harder to pull back out early on in the relationship. As a result, many women stay in relationships even though they saw all the red flags right at the beginning.

Maybe you had a similar experience as I did, that even though you made sure you picked a different type of guy every time, your experience of being in the relationship was similar in each. Maybe you concluded that given that possibly something is rigged against you and it is just never going to work out for you?

Granted, creating a great relationship seems easier for some than it is for others. I promise you as you dive deeper into this book you will find out why and what you can do about it.

Let's check in first, though, to see what have your relationships looked like this far.

- Have you been pursued by guys who are overly attentive, super nice, kind of like a dream-come-true at first, and then after some time, they went missing and became totally aloof and emotionally unavailable, giving you lame excuses and being elusive and evasive?
- Have you found yourself getting into a relationship and before you knew it, you found yourself in a constant war zone – lots of arguments so you were constantly fighting back about accusations that you found were unfounded and so forth?
- Have you felt suffocated by your lover's attention and possibly neediness and constantly felt like you had to look for a hiding place, making up stories just so you could get away and create some space for yourself to breathe?
- Have you been the perpetually abandoned one? You gave everything you had; you tried to find new ways to show your love, proved your dedication, yet all you got was this flimsy commitment, if any, in return.
- Are you usually the one who is to blame for all that is going on, and although you do believe you contribute to the failure of the relationship, nothing you ever do is

- enough or brings about a desired change, and the long-awaited closeness never comes about?
- Maybe you have found yourself to be with a psychopath who simply wants to use you and has been lying to you since day one, and you were lucky to get out in time.
- Or maybe you have been in one or more relationships where there has been overt abuse, such as physical and/or sexual abuse, on top of the emotional and mental abuse.
- Or have you been avoiding relationships altogether and chose to go solo all this time; which has its plus and minuses?

There has probably been some combination of the above to varying degrees, and I am so sorry that you had to go through any of them. The heartache, confusion and wasted energy can be so frustrating and painful.

Emotional intimacy takes time, gentleness, honesty, and much courage. Emotional intimacy encompasses honest and vulnerable communication about one's own needs and feelings without making the other person responsible for them. It takes the willingness to really hear and understand a man rather than hoping the knight in shining armor will fix everything with his superpowers. It takes a lot of self-trust to create a space for a man to feel safe so he can connect with his feelings and needs and communicate them. All of that is a lot more uncomfortable and vulnerable than having sex.

As you may know, we live in a universe governed by the law of attraction which means that the vibration we hold in our being, conscious and unconscious, creates our reality. The problem is that we are not entirely conscious of how and what we create.

As per cognitive neuroscientists, we are only conscious of about five percent of our activities, such as our feelings, thoughts, and automatic behaviors. This means that we are not conscious of about ninety-five percent of what is driving, motivating, and informing us. I find that quite worrisome, and it goes a long way in explaining why we might not be in total control of what types of relationships we end up in because, after all, how do you know what within the ninety-five percent creates your relationships?

These numbers are an easy explanation as to why you might repeat similar relationship experiences even though you might have tried really hard not to do so.

There are specific points in time, specific events, where the energies responsible to create happy, intimate relationships went out of whack. The good news is that the approach I discovered allows you to sift through the ninety-five percent of "stuff" buried in the subconscious quite effectively and zero in on the ones that affect relationships the most. It is like picking up a laser beam to connect with what went wrong and make it right now in the present moment.

It is helpful to become totally clear what the old paradigm was that you created former relationships out of. You need to know what the old operating system was so you can consciously design a new one and then make the switch.

- What were the emotional needs behind your actions that drove and motivated you? Did this approach work in meeting those needs?
- What were the beliefs that you held that informed your decision making?
  → Beliefs about men
  → Beliefs about what you deserve
  → Beliefs about what is possible in relationship
  → Beliefs about what is normal
- What were the assumptions you made about yourself and men in general?

- What have you learned from your environment growing up that you applied without questioning?

You need to become meticulously familiar with what that old paradigm was all about so you can slowly start to disassemble it, and simultaneously, you need to let yourself dream, visualize, conceptualize, what it is you do want, what you do long for, how you truly want to feel about yourself and life when you are in a relationship. You need to know the old so you can detect it when is shows up, and you also need to have the new readily available at your fingertips to refocus your mind and give it direction.

Most women with whom I talk about this need much support to even stay on topic. Most women are really good at describing in painstaking detail what went wrong; however, they can hardly articulate what it is they want. They constantly change topic, and I have to bring them back to the question: What is it that you do want?

It almost seems as if it hurt the brain to articulate or think of what it is they want, as it has never seemed to be an option to have it. It is new territory, and the brain doesn't seem to be able to focus on it for more than ten seconds at a time. The grooves in the brain that have been noticing and counting the dysfunctional ways are deep. Carving out a new groove that is about seeing a new way takes real effort and concentration. It is so natural to constantly reference what was and what still hurts.

Yet without making the effort to articulate and visualize what it is you do want, you will actually never be able to manifest it.

Identifying the old and the new paradigm are essential tools for moving from the old to the new. And what you are about to learn in this book will give you invaluable tools on how to dissolve the old paradigm and create a new one.

There actually is a method to this madness – the madness being your painful and frustrating relationships. How many times have you been certain that this time will be different? This time you found the right guy. And yet again, did it turn out a similar way?

If you are up for it and you have nothing to lose, I'd like to share with you this system of rewiring the old relationship-forming hardware that brought about profound and lasting change for my clients.

Chapter 6

The Secret Maps

"Real liberation comes not from glossing over or repressing painful states of feeling but only from experiencing them to the full."
– C.G. Jung, *TheAarchetypes and the Collective Unconscious*

As I had mentioned earlier, I am also going to share with you about the phenomenon and power of the archetypes.

You may have heard of archetypes before. Dr. Carl Jung, a world-renowned psychiatrist from Switzerland, coined this term. First of all, you have to know that Carl Jung went to the same university as I did, and he spoke English (you can find videos of him speaking English on YouTube) in just the same way as my grandfathers did. I have a soft spot for him in my heart and admire his tremendous courage and deep attunement that he needed to have had to make the discoveries he made and to complete his life's work. I adore him.

Jung realized that every civilization in any given time period had identified the same types of forces and energies governing the human experience. Each epoch, each time period, each culture, each tribe, each society had an expression of the same archetypal energies. They called them differently, and they depicted them differently; however, Jung found that they were all tapping into the same energy. And each archetype represents a different set of energies. These are innate energies that govern our limited human experience, the realm of the human expression where we have personalities, needs, conflicts, hopes and dreams.

Jung also identified that each archetypal energy looks and manifests one way when it is integrated and also looks a different way when the person has not yet made a conscious connection with it and hence is living out the experiences of the shadow aspects of the archetype. In fact, the Greek tragedies are all based on the concept that humans are bound to live out the shadow aspects of the archetypal energies and can never not do that.

What fell into my lap on that cold winter day seems to be a way to crack that predicament. We can, if we want to, defeat the premise of living in an ongoing, never-ending Greek tragedy.

The information about the archetypal energies I will share with you from here on forward is based on my own work and my own experience of diving deep into these realms. I have used the information compiled by Robert Moore and Douglas Gillette in their book *King, Warrior, Magician, Lover: Rediscovering the archetypes of the Mature Masculine* and then researched the feminine counterpart to their book. It seems that nobody has yet written that book, which was a key reason for me to write this book. Naturally, I can't compare my book with theirs; I see it more as another facet, another angle.

I gleaned the main components of the feminine mirror image of the book mentioned above and then put it to test when working with my clients.

As I applied the information that Robert Moore and Doublas Gillette shared in their book to the process of releasing emotional trauma, the whole phenomenon of the archetypal energies became alive for me.

As much as I adore and respect Jung and his work, I found his books and those of his students quite boring as they were so theoretical. For me, information has to be relevant; it has to be applicable, and it has to produce results. I am not a scientist nor a psychologist.

I did glean the overarching models and concepts from those books and then applied my own way of doing things, which lead me to fruitful discoveries.

I am deeply fascinated by human nature and love us tremendously, and I am driven to find new ways to understand and relate to what creates our realities and how varied each of our realities are. As I dove into this process, I had the first-hand experience of the astounding truth of the archetypal energies. They are indeed a shared experience; they are indeed a phenomenon that is repeatable, manifesting virtually the same in all people, no matter their upbringing or their cultural or religious backgrounds.

I soon noticed that diving into one archetypal energy within one person revealed the same physical symptoms, the same suppressed emotions, the same motivations, as in every other person I worked with approaching that same archetypal energy. It has been quite a fascinating ride.

The information you are about to read is not a result of a scientific study, nor has it been copied from anyone else's book; it simply is a compilation of my own observations and experiences working with the integration of the archetypal energies in my clients.

Each energy comes along with its specific wounds, hopes, and dreams, and there is a clear map embedded in it all that shows us the way as to what needs integration so a new underpinning for our relationship dynamics can be formed.

The archetypal energies indeed are real, powerful, and we all share in the experience of them. The shadows too are real, and we too share the emotional and mental structures of how they manifest.

Hence much of our human experience is indeed shared, similar, and sometimes downright the same, even in areas of our lives where we feel that it is impossible for anyone else to feel or experience the same. I find it endlessly fascinating how similar and different we are all at the same time. That is one reason why I started to work with groups of people so they could see that their most intimate, well-kept secret was indeed not a secret at all. Instead, those key experiences are endlessly shared, and once we connect with that, a huge weight of shame usually drops away, as we generally feel ashamed for the burdens we carry around and the fact that we are still carrying them.

I have come across in some of the books that there is this idea that any given person is governed more so by one specific archetypal energy than another. And although there may be truth to that, I like to think of the varieties of the archetypal energies as an opportunity to become a really well-rounded person. Integrating all archetypal shadows brings about a sovereignty that we all would enjoy and derive great benefit from.

Jung also coined the term of the Collective Unconscious. The way I see it in my minds' eye is a deep ocean or enormous lake underneath the surface of the earth that contains all the emotional and mental conditioning and programing of all humans who have ever lived on this planet. It is like an underground lake of information that informs us deeply how we feel and act and think, and we have no idea that it exists and that we are hooked into it by default.

We are all connected to that Collective Unconscious by virtue of being human. We don't get to make a conscious choice to login when we are born; we simply are logged in as part of taking birth on this planet. The problem with that is that in that underground lake there is a lot of stuff that we are tapped into that does not serve us – not if we are looking to create relationships with humans that are based on win-win, that are based on true connection, love, and respect. The Collective Unconscious has been loaded up with patterns that cause dysfunction and pain.

The concept of creating win-win relationships within and without, collaboration, connection, mutual support is not yet loaded up into the Collective Unconscious to a degree where it would be easy to tap into it. It is there but still faint, and every human who takes it upon themselves to deeply change up their own wiring does affect the entirety of the Collective Unconscious. When you do any work to uplift yourself, you change the pool of information held by the Collective Unconscious.

If you know anything about the history of humankind over the last few thousand years, you know it was not pretty. The emphasis has not been on taking care of each other, building deeply connective relationships, or advancing and honoring the human potential. The emotional states and mental patterning that this caused is stored in the Collective Unconscious as a baseline.

Becoming aware of what is stored in the Collective Unconscious helps to understand things like a fifty percent divorce rate in the USA. As a whole, we have not yet rewired ourselves to do relationships that honor who we are as individuals and promotes deep connection and belonging.

There is a close link and sometimes an overlap of what are ancestral and what are archetypal patterns. Our forefathers and mothers too have had their share of acting out on the archetypal shadow patterns, and so we get that version handed down as generational patterns, and also of course, it is neatly recorded in the Collective Unconscious as well. It seems as someone is making sure we get hammered one way or another.

Another fascinating aspect of the work with the archetypes and their shadows is that these energies are always buried in the subconscious. I was anticipating proving that wrong in my own experience and have to report that up until now it has not been the case, not one single time. Each and every time we connect with a shadow aspect, it turns out to be an experience the person had not yet been aware of no matter how much personal transformation work they have already accomplished. On that note, I'd like to invite you to read the next few chapters with great curiosity and openness.

Before we dive in, one archetype after another, let me give you a little bit more of a framework so you can organize it easily in your head as you read along.

The archetypal energies are composed of a child and an adult version. In psychology, they refer to this as the immature and mature versions. I find that a lot of terms used in psychology do not land well with my clients. Who wants to be called immature? Also, the terms used for the shadow aspects of the archetypes and even the archetypes themselves I don't always find so fitting, and sometimes downright offensive. For that reason, I have changed a few of them in my own use and also here in the book.

So the child, or immature, version of the archetypal shadows is one set of shadows, and then there is a mature one. The child version is what normally in a trauma-free childhood would integrate naturally. The adult version is what normally would integrate in adolescence if there was a trauma-free first eight years of life.

The other distinction is that each archetype has a masculine and a feminine version, and each person, whether male or female, has both archetypal energies and benefits greatly from integrating both, the feminine and the masculine. When you integrate both the feminine and the masculine version of the same archetype, you will feel and know from the inside out what these energies feel like and what is becoming available to you in form of new behaviors and emotional and mental patterns.

Please know that it doesn't matter of what sexual orientation anyone is. Some men are more in touch with their feminine energies and vice versa. I am going to speak out of a heterosexual perspective for simplicity.

Now let's dive into all four of the key archetypal energies and look at how they govern our experience, both in the masculine and feminine versions, as well as the child and the adult versions.

Chapter 7

Connection, Connection, Connection

"A woman's highest calling is to lead a man to his soul so as to unite him with Source. Her lowest calling is to seduce, separating a man from his soul and leaving him aimlessly wandering. A man's highest calling is to protect a woman so she is free to walk the earth unharmed. Man's lowest calling is to ambush and force his way into the life of a woman."

– Cherokee Proverb

My favorite archetype is the Lover archetype. I like to call the Lover archetype the archetype of Connecting. The Lover archetype insinuates the exclusive, romantic, and sexual relationship with a significant other when really I have found that the Lover archetype energy governs all relationships, all ways of connecting: the one with self, the one with any other person, with nature, with animals, with all that is.

When the energies of the Connection archetype are fully integrated in a man and a woman who are in a relationship, meaning they are not run by any of the shadow aspects, it would look something like this: The feminine has the role of leading the masculine deeper and deeper into his own inner world, his own inner mystery. The inner mystery is naturally part of the feminine, she is at home there. She knows her way around. She is deeply intuitive, connected to her emotions and all that is. She is the perfect guide to bring the masculine to discover this within himself. You can only imagine how much trust there would need to be. It requires a level of trust that most modern couples do not have. In fact, most modern couples operate on a different premise.

The goal of the feminine leading the masculine deeply into his own inner world is so that he can connect with all that is because now he can connect with himself. This adds a mystical dimension to his life and makes everything more vibrant, relevant, and precious. The feminine becomes the masculine's ticket to knowing and feeling all, and by virtue of living in this way, his ways of moving through life now become informed by benevolence, infused by a wisdom that everything is connected and equally valuable. There is a deep union and trust when both the feminine and masculine meet in the space of the Connection archetype, a sacred alchemy indeed. When you look at relationships in this way, it becomes apparent that the ideals of marriage that modern man has adapted to are quite different in purpose and quality.

The union between the feminine and masculine within the Connection archetype is one where both have endless space to be who they truly are. There is not pushing or pulling; there is no demanding or criticizing. I have had clients say to me how astonished they were by the seeming paradox of how connected and how free they felt both at once after a full integration of the connection archetype. There is what you could call interdependence – a state that honors the belonging but is not codependent. It is a beautiful dance that is led by the music of the soul. It is not what some might call independent, as it relates, takes care of, and is deeply connected.

When Marta first came to me, she wanted me to help her tap deeper into her creative flow as a theater director. It was something she was passionate about – so passionate, in fact, that she denied herself the desire to be in a relationship. Her sole focus was to fully embrace her artistic expression and to take that to the max. Avoiding relationships was a part of her strategy, as she knew it would totally throw her off and render herself incapacitated.

She kind of avoided the topic of relationships altogether; it was a terrain that scared her. Naturally so, as her association with being in a relationship was that of getting stuck in a disempowered, dark place. She was determined not to go back there. She figured that if she dove fully into her artistic career, she could somehow avoid getting into the messy terrain of relationships.

When I inquired more about what she really wanted, she mentioned a faint wish to maybe one day be in a relationship. She even added to maybe, possibly, one day, have children. Later she shared with me how in that moment of sharing this with me, she was overcome with deep shame, as if wanting to be in a relationship was inherently wrong.

In a workshop about creating deep connectedness in Warsaw, Poland, Marta allowed for a deep transformation to take place that shifted the way she experiences being in relationship with a man completely. She hasn't been the same since. She owned her deep desire of wanting to be with a man and allowed herself to feel and express the shame she felt about that, and coincidentally, in that workshop, she met a man. And thus, her career-oriented life suddenly turned into the most amazing, heart opening love story.

As I supported Marta, she dropped her fear of losing herself and of getting stuck in that dark place. She quickly learned how to be truly vulnerable in a relationship and trust herself and her partner in a way she had never experienced before. She got firsthand proof that she could be deeply engaged in a relationship while also being fully or maybe even more so present with her art. She learned the art of creating emotional intimacy and protected that space with great vigilance. She did not allow anything to linger or pollute the sacred space of her relationship. She learned new skills on how to communicate and address what needed to be resolved, and each effort brought them closer.

In the process of integrating the feminine archetypal energies that we will dive more deeply into in this book, Marta connected with a powerful feminine energy within her and blossomed. So did her relationship. She allowed her man to support her – a concept that had been looked down upon by countless female generations before her. She came from a people that had undergone countless and ceaseless wars and strife, and this taught the women not only of her lineage but of her country to always be on guard and always be self-sufficient from a man. Being dependent on a man in times of war when men are called to battle and other men invade your country, as you can imagine, never ends well. Women were required to be strong, which in this instance meant masculine.

The more Marta allowed the feminine energy to become a dominant experience, the deeper the relationship became and the more relaxed and energized she became. It unfolded really fast, and within weeks after the workshop, she found herself in a totally different relationship terrain, a terrain where she embarked on a relationship path full of love, trust, beauty, and connection – something that truly had not been possible for her prior to the workshop and sadly not for any of her female ancestors. It felt as if she rewrote her country's history at a cellular level. It felt daunting to her, as it was completely uncharted territory, and it required a lot of trust in herself to allow this new way of being to unfold. I supported her along the way in opening up to these new ways of being, resolving old hurts and angers that felt so ancient they were hardly her own.

Marta shared that one of the most beautiful things she gained from having worked with me is that the connection between her and her partner is deep yet, at the same time, they both feel free. They grant each other the space to be who they truly are and the space they both need to grow, an experience that was the complete opposite of what she was so afraid of. In fact, she says that this has been the most beautiful experience of her life.

Not too far into the relationship, Marta asked me for support with getting pregnant. That took hardly any time, and I assisted her and her partner in integrating the Mother and Father archetypal energies, for obvious reasons. Marta was able to activate a way of being as a mother that was completely different from what she would have naturally inherited from her mother. Through the integration, an old fear that felt as if it came straight from the Collective Unconscious reared its head. A deep fear of being unsupported, abandoned, left to fend for herself, melted into a deep, warm place of feeling totally supported not only by her partner but by everyone around her. Marta felt how deep that sense of being unsupported runs in women as a whole, and she could see it in her friends and female members of her family; she felt really lucky that she was able to turn that experience around for herself and step into a whole different feeling space within. In turn, she was able to be fully present with her unborn child for whom connection is as important as it is for an infant.

The most amazing part about it all for her was that not only did she find and connect with her true love and get pregnant, but she also excelled in her role as theater director. In fact, she found that the new ways of being in a relationship and in becoming a mother added so much more depth and meaning to her professional work. She created a truly interdependent relationship that allowed both to fully be who they were, and not only that, they both had room and space to grow into who they were and wanted to be.

When people connect with this energy, they literally start to feel less alone and less isolated. This shift takes place without there being any change in the actual circumstances or in the people around them. There is a sense of belonging and connecting that starts to take place from the inside out quite naturally. It feels really good, and people love deeply enjoy that. It is deeply relaxing to feel belonging. And strangely, belonging, is an inner experience, even though you would think that feeling really would depend on other people's behaviors toward you. So far, this feeling of belonging has become available in each and every session focused on the Connection archetype.

Susan, a client of mine, shared with me that after she had integrated the connection archetype energy in a workshop with me, she noticed that doing her regular day-to-day life took way less energy out of her; it dawned on her how afraid of people she had constantly been and how much energy she had to exert all the time to manage that fear. After the integration, Susan not only had no need to exert that energy, but she actually felt energized and enlivened by doing activities that involved being in places where there were lots of people. A totally new way of living opened up for her. Susan no longer needed to scan and read everyone's energy around her to gauge whether she is safe or not. All of a sudden, she realized how many caring and loving people there are in the world, ready to connect and share their love.

Depending on how severe the emotional trauma in relation to the caretaker of the opposite sex has been in childhood, the feeling of connection is affected.

Let's start with the feminine version of this archetypal energy. When the relationship between a father and his daughter doesn't go quite ideally, the natural integration of this energy is hindered and hence will not be available as an experience to this woman as she grows into an adult. The extent of this trauma of course varies in severity in every person's life. It becomes a direct indicator of the degree to which this woman will be able to feel connection and belonging. You may remember that I said everyone has both the masculine and the feminine version of each archetype.

The trauma can look like a father who is emotionally unavailable but physically present. Or it can look like the father who is physically not present, as the parents are separated or divorced. It can also be that the father is present, but he does not respect the emotional and/or physical boundaries of his daughter. He may be emotionally, physically, or sexually intrusive and/or abusive. This spectrum between total absence and total intrusion by the Father energy forms the trauma, which then informs to what degree the energy of the connection (Lover) archetype becomes available to this person as an adult.

I like to call the shadow pair of the child version in the feminine version the Seductress and Daddy's Little Girl. Even though most of the time that shadow is in the shadow, because it did not get to be Daddy's Little Girl, it still is all about her relationship with dad.

In the masculine version, it is the Dreamer and Mama's Little Boy.

When you move into the adult version, you will find an adult type of both of the same as in the child version, only now it is a little bit more pronounced and a lot less innocent.

In the feminine version, it is the Femme Fatale and the one who is frigid altogether, and in the masculine version, the shadows are referred to as the Impotent and the Addicted Lover.

I find all the terminology falls short in finding a description that both nails the nature of the shadow as well as is still respectful and loving. Often, I find that the names given by Jungians are somewhat judgmental and/or deprecating. And it is the judgment that keeps shadow aspects in the shadow — so I like to always soften it out with my clients. The Femme Fatale is the one who loves to be seductive and enticing to the male. However, what makes her a Femme Fatale versus a femme (French word for woman) is that the man can never succeed in having her. He will always be deprived of actually connecting with her, no matter what he gives her in the form of attention, love, money, etc. Fatale means fatal.

Many of my women clients have adopted a stance of invisibility to avoid drawing the father's attention, as having his attention did not feel safe. They tend to be invisible to their mates and are not able to set boundaries and/or ask for what it is they need and want. This can often translate into feeling uncomfortable when a man is paying attention to them. Another client of mine described how after the connection archetype integration, she completely lost that feeling of being uncomfortable if men looked or did not look. She became completely unaffected by it and realized how much of her feeling unsafe in the world as a woman had to do with her own internal wiring.

Others are stuck in a perpetual trap of trying to reach out to their father, trying to lure him back, getting his attention so as not to be abandoned again.

In fact, the two shadows of the feminine child version of the Connection archetype are the one who is trying to manipulate the father into giving the kind of male attention she needs, and the other aspect is the one feeling devastated and violated by the emotional neglect and/or abuse.

When a woman becomes aware of that part of her that is constantly trying to manipulate the male energy in her life to put her at ease and make her feel safe, dynamics start to shift rapidly. When that part gets to be herself unencumbered, she can show up as a calculating personality. She is constantly trying to assess the risks, the chances of getting her needs met; she measures the distance of the male; she figures and calculates as to how to bring him into right relationship with her – a job a little girl should not have to do, a job no one, not even herself, is aware is being done. This part usually comes up as being somewhat frantic, exhausted, and also feeling utterly ineffective. After all, she never actually gets to arrange the circumstances of her life to the degree where the needs of the vulnerable aspect of her are met. Never.

And so she is trapped in a never-ending, panicky, if not hysterical and draining, activity, having long lost any awareness of what happens and why. When we finally connect with that part, there first is great confusion, as she has lost complete touch with how she got herself into that place. Her stance is that of a determined soldier, one that will never give up, not over her dead body. What that can look like is an active mental acidity that never shuts up, a frantic and anxious energy that never calms down. Connecting with this aspect can allow a woman to relax into herself for the first time in her life. I have seen it happen many times. In fact, I have seen the outline of self-hatred wash away when this integration takes place.

A big shift that usually takes place after the integration is that the love being offered to a woman who is in a relationship all of a sudden seems to be enough when before the integration there was a feeling of insatiable hunger for love and affection, an experience that can be frustrating to both the women as well as her partner.

Self-hatred is the original wounding that actually took place in the other part – the one that was either violated by intrusion or by avoidance. The tender girl simply needs to feel the protective, encouraging, assuring energy of the father. And instead of being protected and loved, she is being left to fend for herself or is being invaded by the one who ought to protect her. There can be an abyss of hopelessness, a chasm of despair that needed to be buried so deeply, as otherwise living on was not going to be an option. That powerlessness and pain had to be covered up with hatred and anger, two emotions that although grave in themselves equipped her with a faint illusion of power to plow through life. Often, when connecting with this aspect, a woman feels unable to move, speak, or think for a while. It sometimes feels as if that aspect is almost dead and has been grazing the edge of death for how ever old this woman is. The graver this place is, the more ferocious the protector aspect is who is busily trying to manipulate the world around her to usher in some male attention.

You may recall that I had shared that Jung stated that these shadows are always buried in the unconscious. This means that you too have a version of this pair. Just think of how powerful it could be if that pair was led to the light so they could release their endless struggle.

Can you start to see how a woman who uses her sexual energy to draw the masculine energy to herself unknowingly yet desperately tries to make sure this other part of herself is not actually dying? That manipulative aspect is going to use anything at her disposal to save this other aspect – no costs spared. It can look like being a mental cook, constantly nagging and arguing; it can show up like a woman throwing around her sexual energy in ways that do not serve her nor anyone else. In fact, it can easily blow up in her own face and backfire, making her into yet another victim.

When you venture into the unconscious versions of the adult version of this stuck energy, it gets even more serious yet less emotional. The child version integration involves connecting with deep emotional distress so it can finally be validated and met with love and compassion. Once the needs of this child version are met, it can get its bearings and eventually grasp that the overall situation has long evolved out of the childhood trauma; it can start to recognize it is part of a bigger whole and realize that it is part of an adult person. What does not work is approaching these aspects with a grown-up mentality. Doing so just causes more harm and makes the aspects come up with more desperate measures that will backfire. These aspects are stuck in a young version of themselves and need to be related to with exactly what is an age-appropriate approach.

Now when we look at the masculine version of this archetypal energy and how it gets obstructed, it takes us into the relationship of mother and son, a topic that can be quite uncomfortable for women to face, yet I have seen that once a woman allows herself to let this sink in, it changes her relationship with her sons, adult or young, completely. And most of all, and most touchingly so, it sets the son free to be close to another woman.

Have you ever been with a man who was not as emotionally available as you wished he was? There is a reason for that. Once you truly understand it, you will never look at a man in quite the same way. And instead of judgment and resentment toward this common tendency, you may have compassion for his deep-seated trauma that caused him to feel like this toward you, even when you had nothing to do with it in the first place.

Often, women with abandonment trauma who had their share of relationships with unavailable men will retreat into some kind of castle where they are all alone with the drawbridge pulled up. They may occasionally look out the window to see if the knight in shining armor may still show up, but they don't have much hope for that left anyway. What they are no longer willing to do is let the draw bridge down, give the guards a day off, and be vulnerable again, unwilling to step into that vulnerable place of allowing someone to see her and offer a willingness to really see the man for who he might be: scarred, scared and avoidant, by all means not a knight in shining armor.

Let's start with some long-standing history, as it is really important and helpful to keep it in perspective. A woman needs emotional connection to thrive; she needs it much more than a man, since that is deeply engrained into the feminine energy. She needs it even more so when she is to be the nurturer of her offspring. Having the assurance, support, and protective energy from her man allows her to safely sink into her feminine energy, where she finds a never-ending supply of emotional nurturance and energy to take care of her children. But she does need that safety net around her that generally can be associated with the masculine energy that provides, puts a roof over her head, and keeps her safe from danger. It is long known that the best way for a man to love his unborn and young children is to take utmost care of the mother. When the mother is impeccably taken care of, she naturally offers the best care to her children.

Now, unfortunately, this scenario is not the norm. Instead, a woman is often spinning her wheels emotionally, mentally, and often also financially, trying to be it all as her emotional needs are not met in her primary relationship with her man, and as there may be close to zero emotional intimacy, she will need to find a different source. There are of course different options, ranging anywhere from female family members, girlfriends, or neighbors; however, if there is no other source, the emotional needs get unconsciously directed toward a son. There is nothing conscious about that, not for the son and not for the mother. Even if she has a decent emotional connection with other people in her life, her inability to be fully attuned to her baby son can have the same effect.

As soon as he exists in her womb, he can become the new focal point. The baby boy, completely attuned to his mom like all babies, senses the needs of his mom when really a baby should not need to put his or her antennas out for their parent's needs. But they are so attuned, that they pick up on everything and adjust accordingly.

A child's survival depends on the caring of his caretakers. Without the caretaker caring about them, they know they will not survive. This is a knowingness imprinted into the DNA of humankind. A baby knows it must ensure at all times that the adult is positively oriented toward it; a human baby will not survive unless it is taken care of by others, and the baby knows that subconsciously. If there is no love flowing from the adult to the baby, the baby will go into a panic freeze state, as it is no longer sure it will survive. For that reason, the baby will always adjust its behavior to make sure, the caretaker has positive feelings towards it. A classic example is that of the "quiet, nice baby" who may not be feeling quiet at all but who knows exactly that if it were to show its terror the adults would turn their back on it.

What does the baby boy do? It attunes to the mother's needs and figures out ways to meet them. Is it safe to have a mother who is drowning in grief? Or one that is livid with anger? No, that is not safe for the baby. Will it find ways to appease, entertain, distract, soothe the mom? Absolutely. Apparently, this can go as far as a baby boy completely abandoning his own emotional needs, as they often are in complete conflict with what the demands are in the emotional ups and downs of the mother. He learns quickly that his emotional expression and needs need to be squashed so he can dedicate his emotional energy to meeting his mother's emotional needs. One of the ironies is that such a son will become a man who is capable to be deeply attuned to his girlfriend's or fiancée's or wife's needs;

however, there usually comes a breaking point where getting lost in her emotional needs becomes a threat to him.

If you have a son, this might sound really offensive or wrong, and you may feel like this is utter nonsense. I totally agree and get that.

Would you be okay with us continuing this conversation, as a hypothetical exploration of this terrain? If so, please, let's continue. The information in this book is designed to assist in accessing new perspectives that might be liberating for one or the other, not to condemn, judge, or box anyone in.

Let me say again that none of this business related to the archetypal energies going underground is a conscious affair – not for the child and not for the adult. It is part of the human norm and thus just really part of what we are all accustomed to.

The sad part is that these boys – not all of them, just some – end up feeling somewhat like their mother, or the feminine, swallows them up alive and being in close relationship with a female, meeting a female's emotional needs, leads sooner or later to their own extinction. If you have to deny your own emotional needs in order to meet someone else's, it does feel over time as if you are dying. You don't exist. You are nothing. And once a man can extract himself from this experience, he will fight tooth and nail not to get back into it. And that is exactly what it starts to feel to him once he gets emotionally involved with a woman. It may well be the love of his life. It doesn't matter. Dying is worse than anything; dying is not optional. And for the subconscious programing of such a man, being close to a woman equals being swallowed up alive. Mind you, no behavioral adjustment on the adult woman, the wife, the girlfriend who is in his life will make a difference. This fear runs the show or rather the shadow, completely void of any rational thinking, and it fights for dear survival.

There is only one way out of this, and that is for this man to connect with his aspect that did get swallowed up by mom. He needs to be rescued, literally. He needs to be reached, validated in this excruciating experience that has been the epitome of loneliness and fright. This demands utmost care, as much time as is needed and a really good knowledge of that inner terrain. Once this shadow understands where it is trapped, you can lead it out of the entrapment, and the man becomes free again to love deeply.

I have met quite a few men, married and single, who struggled with not being able to be close to women even though they really wanted to.

I have assisted many men with connecting to this part of them. This part is called the Dreamer; I like to call him the Escape Artist. He always manages to get out; I have found them hiding in different galaxies, hovering in a different dimension, hanging out with elementals, in fantasy worlds, you name it. They are traumatized aspects and kind of behave like feral cats. You can hardly touch them, if at all, and you have to be gentle with them. You need to gain their trust, and once you have that, you can help them get their bearing of what has been going on for them at some point far in the distant past and help them understand that the present moment is no longer fraught with the same peril. Eventually they warm up and become aware of their conscious self and then join up with their conscious self and reintegrate. When that happens, a man's relationship experience is changed in the most profound way, in a lasting way. You can't make it undone, as the adult can no longer be traumatized in the same way as did the child; it is not possible to reverse it.

It is not always the case that the mother looks for the emotional connection from a son; simply being unattuned to the son's emotional state can be enough to create this same dynamic, just to a milder degree – meaning that if the baby boy is sad, and we relate to him as being annoying, then we do not attune to his needs and are not meeting him where he is at emotionally. A baby needs to be met energetically, where it is at emotionally, for him to develop a strong and healthy sense of self. When that fails for any reason, he starts to adapt and eventually feels like he cannot be who he is and fit in. In other words, this trauma happens quite easily and frequently, without there being a whole lot of stress or seeming neglect in the mother.

Whenever we do not allow a baby to exist as who it really is and project onto it, we create an isolation between his and our own experience.

Apparently, we have unconscious aspects that really had a rough going and now they run our relationships. Is there any surprise we as a civilization are a little handicapped in this arena? I don't think so. And the really great news is that when these specific emotions that have been stuck since forever are being released our ability to connect changes on a dime. It literally does.

You are so deeply connected in relationships, even when things are really rough, that you still are deeply energetically intertwined. When one person releases one aspect of the trauma that has kept their relationship in a sad and never-ending spin, the other person often energetically follows suit without having any clue that this is even happening.

Another phenomenon that goes along with this is that this relationship with the mom is total taboo. The boy knows he has no right to stand up to her, to break out of this unspoken agreement that he will do everything he can to meet her needs. And I can't begin to tell you about the intensity of suppressed and disowned anger there can be hidden underneath this arrangement. Oh boy. Once this aspect receives validation that his experience is real and not fair, it can start to get its bearings. And often, the release of that anger can be part of it, and it is not a picnic.

For the most part, the manifestation looks like a man who is distant; he may be into sports, a hobby, work, anything that gives him a justification to be away from the dangerous man-eating female. Sometimes they conveniently arrange having to work in a different city or work late a lot, travel, et cetera. Unconsciously, he creates a way out, and the woman feels that, and guess what? It drives her nuts. It usually plays right into the deepest, mirroring wound, that of the abandonment trauma. It activates the shadow in her that tries to rearrange her environment, the people in her life, particularly the men in her life, to somehow meet her needs. It is all fueled by a deep fear that this overwhelming powerlessness will surface again and that she will be so paralyzed she can't move on with life.

She fights. She can get catty. She can get nasty. She may start to criticize and nag. She may start to act and speak in an emasculating way, all in a frantic, hopeless attempt to keep him around and not to fall back into her abyss of abandonment trauma.

At this point, it may be good to remember when I say "she" and "he" it really only refers to the masculine or the feminine. This can be an experience that either a man or a woman has. The tragic part of these archetypal shadows is that they mirror each other and that the woman with the shadow of the wounded Daddy's Little Girl will most likely attract a man into her life that has a severely wounded mama's little boy shadow.

Sounds tragic? Well, there is more. Remember the Greek tragedy? This is what they were talking about. It truly is tragic, and if you don't know your way out of this, you can't get out of this. You can only give up and live in isolation and tell yourself you never wanted a relationship in the first place, not to mention the pain that will either be felt or stuffed under.

The result of the unintegrated Connection archetype shadows in the masculine version ends up being enmeshment trauma, which leads to the avoidant attachment style.

The result of the unintegrated Connection archetypal shadows in the feminine version ends up being abandonment trauma, which leads to the anxious attachment style.

When both versions are activated in a person, the disorganized attachment style ensues.

When you start diving into the adult version of the Connection archetype, it gets quite hazardous. The disaster called women and men in intimate relationship will become so much clearer to you. And better yet, once you integrate these energies at a deep level, you actually have a paradigm shift so powerful that you can never be the same again in relationship.

As I mentioned in the previous chapter, every archetypal energy has a child and an adult version. Integrating the child version is always a matter of working with deeply, suppressed, painful emotions each and every time. That is simply because the events that block the child version of the archetypal energy from integrating naturally during childhood are all related to emotional trauma. Between age zero and eight, a child primarily operates out of a framework of emotion, not rational thinking. Whatever happens in a child's life is experienced as an emotional event. And when these events are not accompanied by a loving and kind adult to assist the child in fully moving through the emotional all the way, the emotion gets stuck.

When we move onto working with the adult version of the archetypal energies, we deal with a different layer of the same energy as we had encountered in the child version. Now we are looking for points in time where the natural integration of this process was interrupted or made impossible. And by virtue of that not being in childhood but adulthood, we deal with a much more powerful experience that comes along with a demanding attitude of having to grow up. The integration kind of yells at the person, "Grow up! Take responsibility for this!" The process is usually way less emotional but not less demanding.

In order to integrate the feminine aspect of this energy, which ideally is done by women and men, the following shadows need to be connected with. One of them is totally disconnected from her sexual energy and is usually feeling deep shame of her physical existence and considers having any physical contact with others as disgusting or revolting. It is not a black and white kind of scenario, but this is the type of direction it usually goes in. The other aspect that needs to be connected with is the one who uses her sexual energy as a means to get men's attention so it can hold their focus and manipulate them for her own enjoyment. This aspect is not interested in actually connecting with men; it just wants to be in control. This is also referred to as the Femme Fatale; we all know her, have heard of her, and seen her in countless movies. She is captivating; she is independent, strong, self-possessed, and at the end of the day, does not care much about her targets (men). Men fall for her and come up empty each time.

There is the perfect counterpart in the masculine version of this archetype. The shadow of the masculine energy, the "dreamer" or the "runaway," in the adult version is the one who drives behaviors such as having flings, affairs, sexual encounters without any emotional strings attached. He does enjoy them to some degree, yet they never serve the purpose of connection. The non-connection component of it is a necessity for it to work. The shadow of the mamma's little boy becomes the Impotent Lover in the adult version. He feels powerless toward women, may act more like a doormat, does not stand up for what he needs, and feels deeply intimidated by women when it comes to intimacy.

Any activity that takes place within the Connection archetype, whether that is coming from a shadow aspect or the fully integrated version, is always about connection.

The underlying motivation is always informed by the desire to connect. Even the activities of the guy who sleeps around, as well as the activities of the Femme Fatale, are driven by the need to connect. Since this is activity within the shadow realm, they are running rogue and are therefore making conscious relationships that include emotional intimacy nearly impossible and for sure difficult.

Both the Femme Fatale and the guy who sleeps around are ultimately protector versions of the shadow aspect that was severely wounded. For the woman it is the frigid shadow, the one who withdrew from even wanting to connect with anyone on an intimate level, and for the men, it is the one who lost his power to the mom and is now feeling impotent.

When Tina started working with me, a deep-seated anxiety if not a downright state of constant panic drove her. It created much chaos in her thoughts, her emotions, and also in her work life.

She suffered from severe mood swings, was somewhat volatile with her work partners, and her life was one chaotic, painful mess. She did not like who she was for others and felt terrible about it each and every single day.

She was also seeing a man who after only a few months of dating managed to turn Tina into his financial support system. He set up the relationship in such a way that Tina felt she depended on him, and although she did not really enjoy herself with him, she stayed and supported him financially.

Not only did she stay in a relationship she did not really like, she also lost herself in this relationship. And one day, she found out that he was seeing another woman. Her world came crashing down. How was this possible? She took such good care of him, did everything he wanted, and now he was seeing someone else?

As a result of our work together, Tina saw that her fear of being abandoned controlled who she was in the relationship. She was unconsciously driven to find a man whom she thought would depend on her and therefore would not abandon her;

hence, having a man whom she had to support financially actually worked for her strategy. This was her way of controlling a man and a relationship or at least, attempt to. She did not actually believe that anyone would ever love her and that the only way to have "love" in her life, was to choose a man who seemed weak, financially and in every other way, so she could take control of the relationship. She came face-to-face with how deeply insecure and unworthy she felt all her life.

Through the integration of the archetypal energies that I facilitated for her, in particular the ones of the Lover archetype, Tina resolved the deep-seated traumas that had her stuck in the illusion that she is unlovable. The notion that she was worthy of love became real. She realized that she is deserving of love and does not have to do or be anything in particular to earn love. She also realized that out of her abandonment trauma she never actually was able to see a man for who he really was. She could always only see a knight in shining armor that was hopefully finally going to rescue her from her demise; and each time it turned out he was not that knight, the world came tumbling down.

Through the integration work, she was able to see a man for who he is – warts and all.

She resolved the anxiety that used to give her fuel for her life and learned how to lead her business, her friendships, and her life in general from a place of genuine love and connection.

I enjoy working with both men and women on both the feminine and masculine shadow aspects in workshops with women and men present. When women watch men move through the integration of the masculine connection shadows, it is as if they start to understand men and their most complex relationships with them for the first time. And vice versa is true as well. The participants are usually speechless, with long faces, looking around at each other going something like, "Oh my, this is finally making sense. Why didn't anyone tell me that before?" Something shifts to profoundly when we understand that about each other (women and men) that cannot be undone.

I hope things are starting to make more sense, and most of all, I hope that this excursion into this territory is giving you hope for finding your beloved.

Chapter 8

Move from Surviving to Thriving

"I have come to believe that in order to thrive, a child must have at least one adult in her life who shows her unconditional love, respect, and confidence."

— Sonia Sotomayor

Thriving. Don't we all want to be thriving? Well, as luck would have it, in our divine design as human beings, there is the innate architecture, also called archetypal energy, that is designed just to do that, to assist us in thriving.

It is composed of a masculine and a feminine component, as all of them are. In traditional psychology these are called the Father and Mother archetypes. They come in real handy. After all, who has not experienced some stress, pain, or disappointment in their relationship with their mother, their father, or both?

In their energetic make-up, the Father energy provides the structure in within which the feminine can grow and thrive. The feminine energy provides the actual nurturance for growth. So if you were a tomato plant for just one moment, imagine that having a really solid Father energy integrated in your being would mean that you have an inner architecture like a tomato cage that is designed to assist you to grow up tall, reach for maximum amount of sunlight, and also the cage ensures that the precious tomatoes you produce not rot on the ground. The nurturance is the water, the nutrients in the soil, the sunlight, everything that the tomato plant needs to produce beautiful, juicy tomatoes.

What I found in my work is that those two energies literally show up in that way. When a woman for example integrates the masculine energy of the Father archetype, she starts to feel like she is supported from the inside out to stand taller, be more assertive in the world, become more able to ultimately provide for herself because after all the core mission of the Father archetype is to provide. The core purpose of the Mother archetype is to nurture.

Interestingly enough, I have found that neck tension, stomach aches, lacking the resolve to take good care of one's self is all tied in with the Mother archetype when the shadow aspects are not integrated. In more severe cases of misalignment with this energy, food addiction and eating disorders can manifest as well. The basic experience we have when the Mother archetype is well and happy within us is that we feel safe, we feel supported, and we feel nourished and relaxed. The opposite is true as well. After integrations of the child version of the Mother archetype, an awareness of being connected to others becomes available. Let's say you have always felt isolated, overwhelmed with work and obligations and your perceived responsibilities to take care, possibly as the sole caretaker of a family member, an entire family, a community, a town, maybe even the world. That is a huge weight on your shoulders, and it does manifest as shoulder and neck tension. When that energy integrates, the feeling of having to do all of that by yourself dissipates, and you start to feel that you are a part of a bigger whole, where there is collaboration available, where there are others with the same vision and goals who want to work together – a paradigm shift from being overwhelmed and isolated to collaborating with others in community.

I have also seen countless times that after this integration self-care becomes a non-issue. It just happens. Good food, appropriate exercise, whatever it may look like for someone, starts to happen on its own accord. It almost feels like a non-negotiable drive that needs to be made way for.

The shadow aspects of the child version of the Mother archetype are the abandoned little girl (abandoned this time by the mother, not the father as in the Connection archetype) and the protector version who is frantically trying to manipulate people around her to take care of her. There is always a protector shadow, trying to meet the needs of the violated one. In the feminine adult version, there is the one who is the martyr and the other one who takes people down, in particular her own children.

In the masculine version there is the highchair tyrant on one hand, and the weakling on the other hand. As that morphs into the adult scenery, it turns more into the outright tyrant who enforces his standards and makes others do things his way to meet his goal of protecting and providing, and the weakling on the other hand who, as the name suggests, feels too weak to do anything. He becomes the doormat kind of dad.

Imagine, you are an eight-year-old girl, and your three-year-old baby sister is being malnourished, abandoned, and scolded by this old witch – and you want to desperately keep her safe, although she is locked inside the witch's house. You are going to try to stop the mailman, the UPS guy; you are going to shake heaven and hell to find someone to finally get her out of the witch's trap. But you can't. That is what it can look and feel like to the protector aspect who is coping for the aspect that has been neglected and abandoned by the mother.

And so it is one more of these never-ending plights of frantic activity and efforts that are all in vain.

Needless to say, this protector version is exhausted as well. However, she is committed. She is determined, and until and unless you intervene in a most loving and understanding way, she will never be able to get off that hamster wheel.

Once you get her off the hamster wheel, and you are able to tend to the battered and neglected vulnerable aspect, you can allow the immense energy of the Mother archetype flow back into your life.

And that my dear will bring about the most amazing, physiological relaxation in your body. No massage can top that; plus, it is there to stay. I had clients report that they were able to discontinue seeing their chiropractor for their regular neck adjustments. Once you no longer carry the world on your shoulders but rather collaborate with others on what needs to be done, the neck can breathe again.

In the adult version of the Mother archetype, we get to meet the parts of us that are moving through life as a martyr and also the one who destroys her children. Yes, I know it sounds gruesome, and it actually is. Let's remember that all of these aspects are unconscious and that they are being counteracted by lots of other unconscious and also conscious aspects of the same personality. So it isn't like you have one full-fledged martyr who only does the martyr thing. Most commonly, these are simply energies working underground, trying to meet their agendas.

We all have these two shadows within us, whether we are men or women, whether we have children or not. One experience all these shadow aspects have in common is that they feel extremely isolated and alone. And most of them feel that they have an insurmountable task or tasks to do, and they don't know how and if they will manage. Let's go easy on them. They are really trying hard, and strangely, they are always working for us. It may not look that way; it may not generate results and outcomes that please us, but deep in their motivations, they are only working for us, never against us. If the results are not what we want, it simply is a matter of connecting with them, learning what they are trying to accomplish and how, understanding their motives and needs, and once they are truly met and seen, start an exploration of finding the win-win version rather than the version that leaves a wake of destruction, pain, or disappointment.

Buried within the shadow of the adult Mother archetype is the tremendous pain and fear of being left alone in pregnancy and in child rearing, if not physically, then certainly emotionally; it is one of the many historical imprints on the human Collective Unconscious. Women, in particular mothers, often do carry a resentment quite close to the surface, and when you lean in a little bit into it, you can find out quickly that they are resentful for not being supported and for being left alone. The resentment can also look like a mad rage. Have you ever witnessed that?

When you understand where it comes from, it becomes quite understandable; when you don't, you might just be frightened out of your wits. If you consider the force of this same experience having repeated itself a billion times and how it all got stored in the Collective Unconscious, you quickly understand why a woman can be so irritable.

When these shadows are integrated, an incredible glow, groundedness, and ease comes about, a certainty of being supported and nurtured that possibly only mother earth can exude quite in that same way. It is that kind of mother earth energy that takes over, that puts the nervous system completely at ease. The results are often feeling deeply supported and a genuine, resentment-free desire to nurture and support others.

The Father archetypal energy on the other hand is much about the structure, the tomato cage, the house, the building, the financial containers. It is quite architectural in feel. It does not seem fancy or alluring, but boy oh boy, does it feel good to activate this in oneself, especially as a woman.

When the relationship for a woman with her dad was not so ideal, that innate sense of "I can make it in this world" is not so strong. The architecture to support financial growth may be wobbly. The self-confidence of "I got this" may be missing altogether. It feels reassuring and comforting to feel that energy in one's own being. I have seen women take their businesses to the next level almost overnight. Maybe they were not able to actualize the next level overnight, but the resolve to do so, which then was the basis for it to unfold in the next weeks and months, certainly did.

A female client of mine, Sophia, was running her own business. She worked hard, was very good at her craft, and her business did alright but not great. Ever since the moment we integrated her Father archetype, the business took on a whole new dimension. She established systems and procedures for her various processes as well as for her finances. It was a little bit like building lots of tomato cages for the things she created to grow up on. As a result, magical things started to happen for her; prospects started hiring her services and bought her products, and partnerships arose that she was always dreaming of. What she had been working for all these years all of a sudden manifested easefully.

And naturally, when men integrate that energy, it has a similar effect. The shadows of this energy are such that they try to accomplish the same outcome with being pushy on one end, compensating for actually feeling completely powerless. One of the masculine shadow aspects feels totally powerless and incapable, and the one is using force to assert and overpower.

When one of the two shadows are active, which is the normal state, then the inner structure for thriving is not available. Once the shadows are integrated, the person will be able to build much more by using the same amount of effort as before because now a structure is in place to allow the growth to thrive.

I find the Mother and Father archetypes quite inseparable. I could not say one is more important than the other, regardless of whether you are a woman or a man. You truly need both to properly flourish.

The one of Father/Mother, or as I call it the archetype of Thriving, correlates to the earth element.

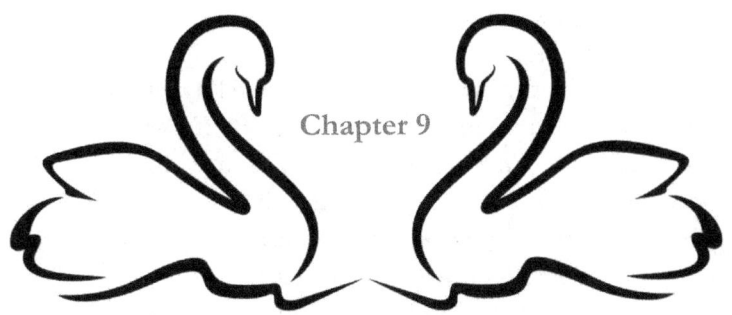

Chapter 9

The Key to Full Self-Expression

"When an inner situation is not made conscious, it appears outside as fate."

— Carl Jung

The archetypal energies that govern our ability to be clear, to have boundaries, to set goals and to meet those goals are commonly referred to as the Warrior (masculine version) and the Amazon (feminine version) archetypes. I like to refer to this archetype as the archetype of self-expression. When this energy integrates, we truly are unstoppable. We are totally clear as to who we are, and we are not holding back the least bit, letting everyone know who we are and what we need. We know where we are heading, and we go there on the direct route – no dilly-dallying, no losing time, no detours, just incredible clarity and purpose.

In modern times, the concept of Warrior can be a confusing one, and that of the Amazon, who shoots at her prey with bow and arrow (and for that reason is depicted in old painting as having one breast cut off so she can aim her arrow better) is not so fitting, I find.

As you know, what matters most to me is what it looks like in real life. What that energy looks like in real life, when it is fully activated, is more like the energy of someone who is fully self-expressed, who has created a life where he or she expresses her gifts and talents unapologetically and has clear boundaries that nurture her/him and those around. He/she has a clear vision and sense of purpose, and goes about manifesting that, in a steady and committed way. Naturally, as you will see when you understand all these four archetypes, these four energies support and influence each other. I like to think of it as that they inform each other. When the Warrior energy is not informed by the Lover, the Thriving, and the Wisdom, then it can get a little harsh, possibly even self-centered.

Whereas if the Amazon/Warrior energy is informed by the other archetypes, it becomes a vehicle for those energies and enhances them, and it also adds a beautiful dimension of what this individual person is all about. There is a perfect harmony between all the four archetypes – the harmony between the aspects that creates community, relationships, self-expression within these relationships, all informed by the inner wisdom and knowing.

Again, like with all these key archetypal energies, there is a feminine and a masculine version, and there is a child version of each of those and an adult version of each of those. And each version contains two shadow aspects.

The feminine versions are the violated girl and the defiant rebel. Who doesn't know them? The violated girl's boundaries were bulldozed right down to the ground and by age eight did not even have a concept of what boundaries are. She is fiercely compensated by the defiant rebel aspect who will storm off and do it all by herself. She will attempt to be independent and self-sufficient for as long as she lives – the only way she knows to protect the violated girl from further violations.

In the adult form, that looks more like the victim and the counter part that is endlessly angry (the Jungians refer to this shadow as the "bitch"). When there are no boundaries, there is a lot of anger. Anger becomes the go-to method for making up for lost boundaries. The angrier a woman is, the more you know how severely the violation of her was.

The masculine versions are that of the coward and the bully to make up for it, and in the adult versions, it then comes to look more like the one who hurts intentionally, an outgrown attempt to protect the one who had to endure pain.

The shadow aspects of all the various Warrior/Amazon aspects are the keepers of anger. You may have heard that in order to access your personal power, you need to get in touch with your anger and transform it. Well, this archetype explains it. The wounding and mostly the protecting of the wound is done with anger. And so in short, wherever you see a lack of boundaries, a lack of clarity or purpose, a lack of the ability to set and meet goals, you are looking at suppressed and/or denied anger that has not yet transformed. Or you may actually be looking at expressed anger that is not being transformed. That of course happens a lot too. But what generally brings amazing breakthroughs is becoming aware of the anger that has been long stuffed away and deemed inappropriate, transforming it.

Granted, that is not comfortable. It can be downright frightening to get in touch with that anger not only because of the anger itself but because of what you have associated with anger, which generally speaking is the reason why it is in the unconscious to begin with. There is so much shaming around anger. And yes, that varies from culture to culture. I dare say that in the American culture, girls in particular but really boys as well are terribly shamed for having anger.

Other cultures do have different degrees of shaming about anger. In general, it is more frowned upon for women and girls to feel anger than it is for men, possibly because the more this energy is suppressed, the less likely it is that this person will come into power, her own personal power. So shaming girls for having the experience of anger is a perfect way to ensure they will never grow into a powerful woman.

Remember, there is a huge difference between feeling a feeling and acting on it. Feeling anger is necessary in order to not suppress it and in order to transform it. Acting out on anger always leads to an injury of connection. It is not necessary to express anger at someone in order for the anger to get resolved. Expressing anger at someone is always damaging. However, feeling the anger, acknowledging it, and finding one's own way to truly and genuinely transforming it allows us to eventually communicate what is essential to another person without the energy of anger. Anger usually comes with amazingly clear messages of what needs and boundaries we have allowed to be steamrolled over. And it is your responsibility to do the work of finding out, layer by layer, what you have overlooked or avoided for which the anger is now trying to make up for. The message that is embedded in anger is always most valuable and needs to be implemented in a peaceful, life-affirming way.

One of my male clients, Alexander, had built a coaching business for men. He was always very passionate about his mission; however, the passion did not always translate into his actions, and his actions did not translate to the results he wanted to see in the world. It was as if he was operating under a glass ceiling of sorts. There were no obvious blocks or emotions or belief systems that were holding him back. In fact, it was a mystery as to why his business had not taken off. He had all the right ingredients.

It was not until he accessed the energies of the adult shadows of the Warrior archetype that his business shifted on a dime. The moment he did that, all of his efforts translated into desirable results.

I find there is great confusion about that. My clients get confused when I encourage them to feel their feelings. As it turns out, no one taught children the difference between feeling anger and acting out on anger. So to be safe, for centuries, children have been told to just make it go away. Eat it up, stuff it down, and let your stomach handle it. It might resurface at some point as an ulcer or worse. But most of all, this anger always has to be shunned away. I have not yet had a client who had learned to be with his anger and allow it to transform in the process of being with it. We generally associate being angry with actually doing stuff out of anger, telling someone "our truth," or breaking something. The truth is that any anger that is acted upon does injure and sometimes downright break connection. And that is the least we need or want. We already live in a rather disconnected human experience; why would we want to make that worse?

In that light, the alternative of stuffing it away seems to make sense. However, that is not necessary, and it is harmful as well. Stuffed-away anger creates a severe disconnect within ourselves. It often looks like harsh self-talk. Abusive self-talk. Self-talk where you can never win, where you are always the idiot, you always loose, and there is no way out. So either way, anger that is not transformed and integrated ends up being toxic to either oneself or to oneself and those around us.

The Warrior in all his glory does not fight out of anger. The Warrior fights, or rather sets goals and meets them, out of knowing who he is, what his values are, what his priorities are – never out of anger. A goal set out of anger and pursued with the energy of anger never brings fulfillment and certainly does no benefit the community at large. It never does.

How does the Amazon transform her anger into power? First, we have to come to the rescue of the wounded aspect of the child version. It is a part of us, the part whose boundaries were constantly violated. They were violated by either being invaded or by people pulling away when they should stay. That is right – boundaries not only get violated when someone barges into our personal space, whether that be with words, actions, or energy. It happens just as much when a person whose role and commitment is to be there for a child pulls away. It is a violation of the connection, the bond, between two people.

And if one of them is a child, the child becomes the victim of the actions of the adult. I hate to break it to you if you are one of the people who preach about not being a victim and who makes other people wrong for acting like a victim. There actually is validity to it in that a child actually is a victim of its environment. And since we as adults are basically populated with countless inner children that are still stuck in various situations where they had been victims, we are in a victim state. The victim no longer is a victim when it got a sincere, loving, understanding leg up. And that is a complex matter. Talking down to anyone about not acting like a victim isn't really helping them to snap out of what is keeping them in a perception of being victimized.

You are four years old, and your mom slaps you in the face. Do you have a choice to pack your bags and leave your family home and go move in somewhere else? Hardly. A lucky situation may be where you literally can go and move in with your grandparents, perhaps. But the majority of situations are such that you cannot leave your parent's or your caretakers' home. You are stuck. And as a kid, you will twist your mind into believing that whatever happens is a manifestation of love. You will believe that if something feels bad or seems bad it means that you are bad. Children never assume their caretakers are bad. We are biologically wired in such a way that we cannot afford that. We depend on our caretakers, and we have to adjust our perceptions such that they are always the good guys.

A child who is abused by their parents will continue loving their parents. The only difference now is that they relate to themselves as someone who is wrong. "There must be something terribly wrong with me; otherwise, they would not yell at me." And so the insidious shame that lives like a never-ending underground river starts to grow. There must be something wrong with me, terribly wrong.

You may wonder how this all ties in with the Amazon and Warrior archetype. There is a particular way in which the initial integration of this energy goes array, and that has everything to do with a child being shamed for their anger, being shamed for the expression of their preferences, being made wrong for having a preference as simple as wanting to wear the pink shirt and not the purple one, and any violation of their boundaries, whether that be invading the child's boundaries or withdrawing from the child. And who has not experienced a parent doing either on a regular basis? When you look at the wounding of the Connection archetype, that is all that we are dealing with there, the parent either pulling away and neglecting the child emotionally and possibly otherwise as well or invading the child, causing enmeshment trauma or physical or sexual abuse.

Cecilia came to seek my help at the end of a relationship, completely heartbroken and confused. She invested her heart and soul into a relationship for eight years that held the promise of marriage. Cecilia's plans were to get married and to build the wonderful and adventure-filled life she always wanted to share with a partner.

Over time, he had pushed her away, further and further out of the intimate circle of their heart connection. He used a nifty way of blaming her for all that was wrong. It was her fault that there was no intimacy. It was her fault that there was no trust and harmony. It was her fault that he had grown tired of her. He went on, and she bought into it.

Without realizing it, Cecilia had internalized being the scapegoat. When her boyfriend employed making her the culprit for everything that did not go well in the relationship, she didn't realize that that was not only an unfair game but an un-resolvable situation. He needed both to keep her and also not to have her close. He kept her on an emotional leash, at arm's length that left her starving for love and affection. She was locked in a lose-lose situation and spinning her wheels to make it better, wondering why it didn't work.

The harder she worked on herself, taking responsibility for what was not going well, the further they drifted apart. She did not understand what happened and why it happened and was pondering how she could have done things differently. She had bought into the fallacy that it was all her fault.

As I supported Cecilia in integrating the archetypal energies, she healed the heartache and despair that made day-to-day life and running a business challenging. She gained perspective of how this relationship with her boyfriend was a reflection of a deep wound that her mother inflicted on her at a young age. Cecilia knew that her mother behaved in ways that some would call narcissistic, a wound that she had been aware of and had worked on in therapy for years but was never able to resolve. Now she could resolve it for herself.

Cecilia also regained her confidence, not only resurrected her business but took it to a whole new level, set boundaries that nurtured and supported her, and cultivated friendships that she enjoyed. She was able to snap out of the illusion that she had to work hard for love, but rather, that she is love and deserves to be loved by virtue of being a human being. Easily said, not so easily done.

Cecilia was able to put the pain-producing patterns of pulling, pushing, manipulating, abandoning, shaming, rejecting, blaming and overtaking into the past. She was able to heal deep wounds that she was not conscious of, such that she can now attract someone who wants the same as her. Connect. Support. Uplift. Enjoy.

Now Cecilia is open and ready for a relationship with someone who can see her and love her for who she is, and she can do the same for him. Her priority is in creating emotional intimacy first where there is trust and understanding going both ways. She is taking excellent care of herself, nurturing her friendships, nurturing her physical and emotional strength. She is also dating, at a gentle pace, taking her time, listening closely into herself and her suitors, this time making room only for what truly honors her and nurtures her.

These are the wounds that need to be resolved before the Warrior/Amazon archetype energies can be integrated, and validating these experiences and allowing these deeply buried wounds to resurface is the groundwork for the effective transformation of the anger and for accessing the tremendous power of the Warrior/Amazon archetype.

Yes, you can transform anger by simply being with the energy of the anger. That is possible. And it moves all that much faster when the events related to that stored up anger can be re-experienced in a safe and guided fashion. Strangely, doing this with care and love can over time give you access to a place inside where stating "no" becomes an easy and loving act.

If you are wondering where your boldness is to do some of the things you have always wanted to do or where your energy is to get out of bed in the morning or why you are so tense in certain situations, this may be a clue. If you find that who you really are in the company of trusted friends or family is totally not who you are when you are at work or with people you are not as familiar with, this can be an indication that your self-expression is actually rather low. And for that matter, you may not be self-expressed around people you are close with either. You may think you know who you are when you are with them, but strangely, you do not feel energized and happy after spending time with them, which is quite a certain clue that you are not fully self-expressed with them either.

Have you ever seen a woman who is all bossy, career oriented and does not seem to care much about others? The power-suit ladies? These are generally women who have brought the beautiful gift of the Amazon into this world and who have not yet been supported to transform that energy out of the shadow of the angry woman into the true and full-on Amazon energy. Once a success-driven woman can make that transformation, the energy that is usually quite off-putting and alienating turns into a gift that benefits all. The Amazon is never just looking out for herself. She is, after all, an embodiment of the divine feminine; hence, she always includes all and looks out for all.

She becomes goal-oriented with a loving focus, with a focus that ensures the welfare of all, such as communities, families, or whole countries. Next time you see a very angry woman in action, just know she is endlessly charged with an amazing potential; she just needs assistance on transforming what lies dormant within her, and she could become the most benevolent force in the neighborhood.

I lead a workshop with about fifteen women and five men. I worked with one of the men in front of everyone, and noticed that the process I led him in was totally stalled. As I felt deeper into what was happening, it became clear that this man was petrified of women, that in spite of his manly, seemingly confident appearance, he was deeply shaking and was terrified to be seen by women. I asked the women to engage in small group work outside of the main room so the men had their time alone to themselves. The atmosphere relaxed immediately and significantly.

To make things worse, the Collective Unconscious connects us. And the Collective Unconscious is loaded with unprocessed anger. When you look at the news, you can see this anger erupting everywhere, in the most expected and also unexpected places. Women have been harboring so much anger over how men have mistreated them for so long. Trust me, it is all stored. And until and unless we as a human race process and release that, it will be there as the knee-jerk reaction experience whenever a man steps on a woman's toe. I would say from what I have experienced in this work with my own clients that the main emotions obstructing good relationships between women and men is anger and resentment from the women's side and fear from the men's side.

As I assisted this man to feel validated in experiencing the fear he actually felt, he relaxed. Being seen for what we feel without being judged can be a most healing and transformative experience, especially since we are used to having to justify how we feel and push back. I leaned in. I validated and empathized with him, which was a new and strange experience for him. He was not used to being seen by a woman in his fear of women. It was the first time in his life where he felt seen and also felt safe, which was so unusual for him that it completely reorganized his perception of women.

After some time of dropping deeper and deeper into relaxation and noticing the fear evaporate, I asked him whether he would allow one or more women into the room. He said yes. I asked him and the other men in the room to identify whom of the fifteen ladies they wanted me to invite back in. It was important to me that they felt they were in charge and were empowered to make the decision versus me as the woman making the decision for them. They simultaneously all picked the same woman.

At first, I was surprised by their choice, as this woman was not the most docile, shy type of woman. Rather, she was quite expressive and had a style of her own. I was puzzled. As she entered the room, and the men connected with her, I got it. They knew they did not need to be scared of her. Why? Because – drum roll – this woman was the only woman of these fifteen women who had done previous work with me and had integrated her feminine child version of the Amazon archetype.

And why did that matter? I tell you why. The unconscious activity of a woman who did not integrate her feminine child version of the Amazon archetype is programmed to energetically castrate men. Yup. I said it. And sorry if I am offending you. But trust me, there is real reason why it is such an immense mess out there between women and men. And nope, it is not just the men. It is an equally balanced mess that we, women and men, bring to the table. It runs deep; it is ninety-nine percent unconscious, and it is a bloody mess.

And there is a reason for everything. The nasty, underground castrating ways of women came about for good reason. Being dominated, abused, and invalidated by men for thousands of years would make anyone furious. Having no overt power, women, clever as we are, found our covert ways to fight back.

Do we own that? No, not yet. As women, we are way too busy blaming men, making them wrong, and holding them responsible for the mess. After all, they created it; we have proof for it. The violation done by men is usually visible and traceable. The violence done by women is usually unseen, and therefore all that nastier, as you can't fix what you don't see or know.

For men, it is no less sticky and icky, trust me. Men have had a choice in the last few thousand years to either be a doormat or the suppressor. Take a look around. How many men do you know who stand in their power, are comfortable with it, and use it to serve humanity, including his spouse and children?

I don't know that many. I know a lot of disempowered men who try to do that and struggle with it big time. And usually they feel really bad about themselves. They have needed to associate that a man being in his power looks like being an overpowering, domineering guy who is insensitive and crude. This has been a historically proven track record. The nice kind of guy, the guy who wants to do good in the world, often does end up acting like a doormat because, for him, stepping into his power looks like being a bad person; he would become like all the other macho guys who are inconsiderate, overpower others, bully others, doesn't care, and worse. So as a nice guy, you don't want to identify with that. You'd rather go the doormat route where you get pretty flattened out from all the walking over you. Ironically, in a way, these two ways of being kind of as a reflection of the two shadow aspects of the Warrior energy. Neither work. Neither feel good. Neither get the job done. The only way for a man to fully own his power and render it into a benevolent force is to own these shadows and integrate them. And that is much easier said than done.

And for the woman, her shadows look something like a defiant rebel who could care less and goes off to do her own, independent thing, completely isolated and alone; she does not get the job done. The other side of the shadow is the one who is completely disempowered, hopeless and powerless, unable to set or uphold the slightest boundary; she does not get the job done either.

She, too, has to integrate all the yucky emotion, dress the festering wounds until they can mend. And then, a new relationship with anger and eventually personal power can ensue – one that serves everyone. As a human race, we are so far from this. It looks like disgruntled, unhappy people who blame everyone else in this world for their misery. A blown-up version of it are nations at war. It is a nasty energy when left to fester, but it becomes the most amazing energy that can literally move mountains in service of humanity when healed and integrated. Do you think it is by chance that so many people do not know what their purpose and direction is in life? That so many people really struggle with having boundaries that nurture them and those around them? It all is tied together in the shadow of the Warrior and Amazon.

If you have ever had to learn how to manage being in relationship with someone who displays narcissistic traits much of the time, you know that setting and maintaining clear boundaries is a key element to success in such a relationship. Without the Amazon/Warrior energies integrated, we literally are incapable of setting and maintaining boundaries without it looking like an ongoing struggle that employs harsh or angry tones to assert itself. Once the Amazon/Warrior energies are integrated, the boundaries come naturally, kind of like a second skin. There is no struggle; there is no "should I, shouldn't I, may I, may I not." It just comes easy and naturally.

What is important to understand about "healthy" boundaries is that boundaries are not walls or conditions. Most of us relate to the term "boundaries" as something that is a hard line, that has to do with possible punishment if crossed, a contraption that keeps us separate from others, when in reality it could not be further from the truth. Boundaries are not a matter of separating ourselves.

Boundaries are a matter of identifying ourselves, our needs, our abilities, our availabilities, for the sake of everyone's well-being. Boundaries have everything to do with knowing in any given moment what works for you, what you can deliver, and what you cannot deliver. A boundary may fluctuate quite a bit from day to day, week to week, even hour to hour. If we have little emotional and physical energy available to us, our boundaries need to adjust to accommodate that.

When we have ample of energy and enthusiasm, our boundaries need to adjust to make room for its expression so everyone can benefit. Boundaries are not solid; they are not rigid, and they are not to keep people out. They are there for you and others to know who you are, what you need, what you want, what you can offer and contribute, and so on. For example, knowing that you are a vegetarian and sharing that with someone as you go about picking a restaurant for dinner is a boundary. It is not a condition and certainly is not pushing the other person away. On the contrary, it gives the other person valuable information on how to relate with you so you both can create a win-win situation. Clear boundaries are a fundamental success factor for healthy relationships that are based on win-win.

In relationships where there is a constant bargaining and pushing and pulling about who does what and why not and over here or but you did this, there is no win-win. Everyone loses, and the only thing we might win is a headache or a tummy ache or just being disgruntled. Having clear boundaries is doing the people around us a favor, as knowing what they are dealing with and how they can interface with you (or not) creates a win-win. When both people in a relationship are clear on their boundaries, it becomes child's play to figure out if, first of all, the two individuals are compatible and, second of all, if they are compatible, it is super easy to figure out how to go about life in a way that makes both parties happy, safe, and content.

When the above-mentioned shadows are not resurrected, taken care of, and integrated, this business of having clear boundaries will always trip us up, not just in intimate relationships but all relationships – business, family, neighbors. I promise you that once these energies are integrated, you will not feel harder or harsher; quite the opposite. There is an incredible softness to those boundaries, as it stems from pure love and respect of who you truly are. It feels delicious, quite frankly. And it takes out all the strife. And yes, granted, with the clarity of boundaries, you will notice that some arrangements in life truly are not in alignment with your essence, and you may feel a need to make adjustments. That can feel like a loss; however, ultimately, it is only a gain. Being in relationships where we are constantly in a tug of war of some kind, we lose energy on a daily basis. When the boundaries are intact for both parties, there is no loss of energy any longer. The two partners only add energy to each other, which makes more than the sum of its parts. I once heard someone say that one plus one is eleven, not two. And I think that is true once the life-giving boundaries are healed and in place.

I admit that integrating the various shadow aspects of the Warrior/Amazon archetype is not for the faint of heart. We have to be willing to deal with tremendous anger and with facing deep hidden hatred that we may have been harboring toward some or all people in our lives. It is not pretty, that is for sure. What is, however, less pretty and downright dangerous and destructive is to allow these energies to continue doing their own thing unbeknownst to us in the subconscious. Remember, just because we don't embrace them with our awareness does not make them go away. They simply do their own thing, in a rogue way, which can look like the self-sabotaging behaviors we do not understand we did. This is definitely one of the integrations that I recommend you do not try at home. In fact, quite honestly, I do not recommend you try any of these integrations at home by yourself. One reason for that is that we are so used to pushing ourselves, rather than hearing ourselves; we want things to move and change, rather than being with and embracing them. For that and many other reasons, I recommend you do not try this at home.

The archetype of self-expression correlates to the fire element.

Chapter 10

Turn on Your Inner GPS

> *"Asking the proper questions is the central action of transformation. Questions are the key that causes the secret doors of the psyche to swing open."*
> – Clarissa Pinkola Estes

What good would all the other archetypes do if we were not fueled and guided by a voice from deep inside us? I suppose not too much. A lover could go astray for a long time, even when all the shadow aspects have been integrated and the deep wounds have been healed, if there is not connection with the inner wisdom; we could still make really poor choices.

Let's say there is a young mother nursing her baby. She is deeply rooted in the energy of the Mother archetype, and she is nestled somewhere in the jungle, leaning up against a large, nurturing tree. She is in total bliss and in harmony with her environment. A tiger approaches. In a split-second, the Amazon energy is activated in her, stands up and with one swoop she takes the tiger down to protect her baby. Had the wise woman archetype been activated in her, she had never gone to the forest in the first place, as she would have known the tiger comes by that area every afternoon.

So each one of them brings something else to the table, and together, it makes this perfect synergy. And not only the four archetypes, but the masculine and feminine version of each, regardless of whether you are a woman or a man. I dream of a time where all humans walking this earth are firmly rooted in all of these energies and have them all available in any given moment. I imagine that to be quite a wonderful time.

One of the shadows of the wise woman/Magician archetype is that of the feeling that you are clueless and actually stupid. We all have that hidden somewhere, and we all have developed various ways of covering up for her. This shadow too is being created primarily by shame. We feel deep shame when we feel stupid. We feel everyone else knows and we don't, and we feel endless embarrassment and shame. We hide this shadow at all cost. The shadow that compensates for this perceived weakness is the one who knows it all. She can come across as arrogant, the know it all, the one who knows better. Always, she knows it better. And if she is not allowed in public, she sure will run your inner dialogue and tell you in the privacy of your own mind how dumb you are, how you should be doing things, and how off you were again.

In the adult version, this looks then more like the know-it-all, and on the other hand, the one who is clueless. I find them to be quite similar in the masculine and feminine versions.

The aspect that feels dumb actually is the one who has the capacity to know, deeply from within, without knowing. And when that part is shamed into oblivion because it does not seem to know normal stuff, we lose access to our inner knowing.

It can sound like one of your inner voices that tells you how you should eat and how you should behave, how you should meditate, and how you should exercise more. And when you don't follow her regimen, you are being harshly criticized and possibly shamed. That all happens within yourself. Depending, you may have a person or two or more (I sure don't hope so) who give you this information directly to your face. Possibly your boss, your mother, a sibling, your roommate? And we can be that way with others as well. Maybe there is one area of life where you are just certain how it should be done and what is better than any other approach.

That is the inner war. The one who feels like she knows nothing at all and who is generally pushed into the oblivion of the subconscious, and the one who then goes to town, believing she truly does know everything and does not hold back sharing. Neither are in touch with inner wisdom. Neither know what is actually going on.

What I found is that by integrating the masculine and feminine versions of the wise woman/magician energies in both their child and adult versions, we connect with a sense of self-worth that becomes quite unshakable. So many clients have reported back to me how all of a sudden, they no longer doubt themselves incessantly or compare themselves. They just know now who they are, and there is a newfound acceptance around that. And in following up with these clients, it seems this has never gone away since then.

When the moment in time where that wound first got created about feeling stupid when everyone else knows is pinpointed and the process of resolving that incident starts to unfold, an ease starts to come over the person. There is so much inner pressure about this not knowing that it can literally be the cause for severe anxiety. Once that traumatic event has been resolved and that aspect is being related with just the right amount of appreciation and encouragement, there comes a moment where it starts to relax and realize it actually does know everything. It knows everything in the not knowing anything. And that is a vulnerable place because we have no control over it. We can't manipulate it; we simply have to be willing to be with the not knowing and then experience what we do know in that moment. That is the knowing. And this part of us that had been shamed way into the basement or below is so good at feeling and knowing the inner wisdom once it is given the permission not to know. This is not just a mental idea you can tell yourself and then it works. No, you have to heal and integrate that part of you that felt like it was going through hell because it didn't know. That trauma first has to be released and dissolved. Then that aspect can naturally tune in and know.

The Wise Woman doesn't only give us access to our inner wisdom and intuition; as if that was not enough, she also governs other areas of our human experience. For example, the wise woman/Magician is in charge of our self-esteem and self-trust. Well, it does make sense that we can trust ourselves much more when the inner wisdom is activated, and once we trust ourselves, we tend to value ourselves more as well. It all goes hand in hand.

I worked with a young artist, Bella, who was passionate about her work and equally insecure about it and herself. She had a way of constantly undermining just about everything she did, second-guessing herself, should-ing herself, criticizing herself, pushing herself to do better. It was relentless, yet her nature was always sweet and gentle, quite the opposite of how she treated herself inwardly.

One day, Bella and I set out to integrate the adult version of the Wise Woman archetype – an archetypal energy we had worked with in the child version some time ago. It was so fascinating to get to know this shadow aspect of herself. Finally, Bella came face to face with this split-off part of her, the part of her that had been task-mastering her with no mercy for most of her life. I lead Bella in a gentle, deep exploration so Bella could get to know and respect her, learn about her motivations, her needs, and her feelings. The irony is that when you take the time to understand anyone or any aspect you do get to see their reality out of which they operate out of, and you discover just how much sense what they are doing makes when you put yourself into their shoes. It was no different with this shadow aspect of her. She made so much sense. Her drive to ensure Bella did all the right things so she could live the best life possible ran deep and strong. What this shadow aspect did not know was that there was a much different way to accomplish the same that would bring Bella so much joy. I assisted Bella on brining this part up to speed – after all, it had been operating in the deep shadows of her psyche for several decades. Of course, she needed some updated information and to get re-oriented to what today's reality actually is all about.

Right after the integration, Bella shared how she felt this new inner space emerge, one of sweetness, joy-filled silence. She said it had become easier to breathe and that the mental activity had slowed down massively. There hardly were any thoughts any longer. Bella even reported that since that integration her difficulties falling asleep at night had dropped away. Instead, she wakes up refreshed and ready to start the day with joy. Bella said that she now wakes up with a heart filled with excitement and curiosity, a feeling she can only faintly remember having had as a small child.

Bella realized that, unbeknownst to her, a force drove her to prove that she was worthy while, underneath it all, feeling despair that she will never be able to prove that she was worthy – true lose-lose setup within the deepest corner of her soul, unaware and yet center stage. This drive determined how she felt in her intimate relationship, in her friendships, toward money, toward her business; all these areas had become expressions of being stressed out over needing to prove her worthiness, whilst knowing she doesn't have any.

On one lovely afternoon when all of that dropped away, Bella realized that she had nothing but joy in her heart toward all those activities. The constant judgment of what was wrong and what was right fell away, and most of her previous thought processes no longer made any sense to her. She realized that the reasons why she had not been undertaking some of her bigger business visions were completely unfounded.

Bella felt so much peace realizing that indeed she was connected with all that is. She realized that what people around her were doing had nothing to do with her and was not a reflection of her at all. And if you knew her, you would know what amazing relief that was for her. Bella also noticed that there were changes in her physiology; she carried herself more upright, and a constant sense of exhaustion that she had carried around with her for most of her life dropped away, just like that.

Instead, she felt an inner sparkling, what she called a "magical, pink, golden creativity" flowing through her that filled her with tremendous joy. And what was funny is that she could no longer conjure up any of the old, nasty inner judgments she had always held against herself when she wasn't living up to par.

You could say that she had the overwhelming experience of her own worthiness. And you know what is the most amazing part about all of this? Months after this integration, it has not changed or reverted to the old setting at all. It has become her new normal out of which Bella now operates.

The wise woman shadow aspects also have quite the hand in creating and thus uncreating disease. As you know, the shadow aspects are never working against us, and they never have an agenda to hurt us or undermine us even though much – not all but much – of what they do can be quite harmful to us and those around us.

You can think of the shadows, regardless of which archetype they are of, like young versions of you that got disconnected and then started running rogue – rogue because they are no longer controlled by your conscious mind. Your mind lost track of them the moment they went into the unconscious, which is at the moment of trauma that created them. They are now self-governing, self-directed, independent agents who totally lost track of the bigger picture. They too no longer know they are a part of you; they don't know they belong to anyone. All they are left with is the original motivation, their innate drive. However, they are set in their ways of doing things at the age of when they were created. For example, they were created in an incident that happened for you at age three.

That shadow aspect that came out of that event is going to be operating at the level of comprehension and awareness of that of a three-year-old, so rough and young. No wonder these shadow aspects seemed to be wreaking havoc. No wonder they looked like they worked against you and that you had to stop them from creating harm. Isn't that most of the time the way we relate to our shadows – a deep urge to shut them up, render them harmless and take them out of the game? This approach I have found revolutionizing in that I could recognize these activities are not designed to harm me; they are actually designed to support me. I just have to make the effort to understand them deeply and be willing to work with them, rather than against them.

What is important is to truly connect with its motivation. The essence of the motivation of the shadow is no different from that of the fully integrated archetypal energy. It has the same drive.

A shadow can deem it helpful to create a disease as a means to achieve something. Let's say one of your shadows thinks that you are not doing the right thing and you are never listening and drawing outside the lines. The shadow might find it helpful to ask your physiology to get tired and sluggish; and that might look like a hormonal imbalance or a low-grade infectious disease. Once you become aware of the shadow and its skewed way of going about meeting its agenda, you can then discover its hand in creating a disease and, along with that, identify that there indeed would be a much better way to accomplish the same outcome. Let's say it was Lyme disease, to keep you out of trouble – trouble that only that shadow aspect perceives as trouble. Then this aspect can release its agenda to keep that disease in place, give a deep message to the brain and the entire physiology to re-think this, and create health instead. I know this sounds wild, but I have seen it numerous times, including within myself. The diseases are usually a chronic condition that wears the body down and deprives it of its vitality.

Once both of the shadows pertaining to the wise woman/Magician are integrated, true wisdom becomes available. A settled feeling of a healthy, self-assured way about yourself becomes available.

The integration of these energies allows us to fully connect with universal wisdom, the power that created the universe, and our ability to align with that so we can co-create.

The one of Wise Woman/Magician, or as I call it, the archetype of inner knowing, correlates to the air element.

Chapter 11

The Keys to Find Your Beloved

"Being deeply loved by someone gives you strength, while loving someone deeply gives you courage."

– Lao Tzu

For me, what matters at the end is that there are results; it has to work, be relevant, and make a real difference. Otherwise, any theory, therapy, or method feels futile to me, no matter how well thought out it might be. I like pudding, and as they say, the proof is in the pudding. Unless there is proof of something providing a massive transformation, it really doesn't mean much to me. The most well-written books that are based on decades of research and learning don't touch me if they do not also bring about a useful change that is important to me or those around me.

Let it suffice to say that I would not entertain these concepts of shadows and archetypes and so on if they did not contain a key to massive transformation. I have no time to waste and have no intention of ever wasting someone else's time.

In my practice and experience, this approach has brought about such deep change in little time. And the more I observed this, the more excited I got.

Let me summarize what we just explored in a practical way so you can assess whether any of this is relevant for you in your day-to-day life because, after all, if it didn't, what good would it do?

Most of all, I find it to be such an incredible relief that there is indeed a method for this madness called intimate relationships. Most of the time, we are in the throes of the confusion, the hurt feelings, the need to retreat, the anger, and the sense of hopelessness or powerlessness. And it basically does all feel like a humongous mess, one that cannot ever be sorted through and resolved. And as a result, we will most likely always suffer a certain degree of loneliness, even when we are with someone.

Once you intimately understand the underground workings of all the shadow aspects of the four key archetypal energies governing the divine masculine and feminine energies and how they interact, trigger and enhance each other, the disaster called intimate relationships actually starts to make sense and even becomes predictable.

There literally is a science to this madness, the science of the missing archetypal integrations.

These dynamics can be truly understood, and when willing to do the deep emotional work, they can be completely resolved. A participant in a workshop once expressed that she now understood that there actually is a map inside herself that is guiding her directly to creating meaningful, connective, happy, healthy, and uplifting relationships.

She literally saw and experienced it as a map – it wasn't just a figure of speech. In a way, you can think of the archetypal world, when not integrated, when acted out through the various shadows, as a terrain for which there is no map to successfully come out on the other end. From what I know now, it is impossible to create happy relationships with these energies being out to lunch. It just is not possible. And as you start integrating them one at a time, this inner terrain starts to change visibly, and paths, even roads, start to show up. What might have been a desert-like mountainous terrain with no paths now is a landscape with rolling hills and wide roads that are easy to travel while you enjoy a spectacular view.

The complexity of the interactions of the various shadows and what they create first within one person and then within a relationship is truly mind boggling and most of the time quite disturbing, hurtful, and undesirable.

Chapter 12

Nothing Will Work Unless You Do

"Nothing will work unless you do."

– Maya Angelou

With great power comes great responsibility. I also think that similarly, when we know something, we can't unknow it, and along with that comes a new level of responsibility.

For example, there was a time where the medical field didn't know that the high rate of infant mortality had something to do with the level of hygiene in hospitals. They had no intention to not solve the problem; they just didn't know what the problem was.

The responsibility to keep the hospitals clean was there but not as crucial. Once they learned that there is a direct correlation between the level of hygiene and the level of infant mortality, the rate of infant deaths became the responsibility of the hospital administrations, and they addressed it immediately.

I think it is not much different with our own quandaries and miseries. As long as you don't know that there is a solution, you are kind of in the throes, and quite frankly, what else should or could you do?

What I am trying to say in a nice way here is that you can sit around and sulk, but you can no longer say you don't know why or how to solve it.

Once you know there is a solution out there for the problem that holds you hostage, you owe it to yourself to solve it. And since we are an integral part of the whole, I do think we actually owe it to the whole as well to solve it. Any human being who decides to make themselves into a happy, thriving version of themselves is uplifting the planetary frequency all by his or herself. You finding your beloved will uplift the world's frequency and also, by shifting your unconscious, inherited relationship dynamics, will update the Collective Unconscious and will therefore make it easier for anyone coming after you to do the same.

It is like using a machete in the jungle to get through it – once a sizable group of people has gone the same path using machetes, soon you can bring in the bulldozers, and before you know it, you have a highway with lots of traffic. Granted, this may not be the most ecologically sound analogy; please pardon me for that. But if you think of the highway as a means where other people can much more easily get from point A to point B – where point A is wiggling out of old and painful relationship patterns, and point B is living in deeply connected and fulfilling relationships – then you know what I mean.

In particular, I'd like to address a touchy subject which is the entitlement of women to blame men for bad relationships. Somehow, we inherited this long-standing righteousness of pointing our fingers at the lousy husband who runs off with another woman, abandoning his wife and children, or any version of the same popular images we hold in the Collective Unconscious. Or the guy who is the hopeless doormat, whom we disrespect and walk right over, conveniently too weak to stand up to our bossy demands. Or the guy who is bossy himself, violent possibly, having no concern or empathy for anyone else's needs and feelings or some odd combination of the latter.

We are in this picture. And whatever picture we are in, we co-created it. Granted, it may have been our fore-mothers who co-created it and then handed it down to us; however, we still are in the picture and therefore perpetuating it. Whatever problem we perpetuate, we are not solving. And it is time to solve it.

We live in a time where much is being rewritten, reformatted, and reevaluated. The way we do medicine, the way we do education, the way we do agriculture, the way we do electric power – everything is being looked at through a new set of lenses, a new lens that has the intention to honor mother earth, honor the true needs of a human being, and eventually support the human race to evolve into its full potential, living in harmony will all of creation.

Let's summarize the key points of each archetype and then go into how they affect and influence each other because you may be wondering how the energies of the archetype other than the lover/connection are affecting your ability to have strong, happy, and thriving relationships.

The Archetype of Connecting, Also Known as the Lover Archetype

This is the key archetype in regard to relationships. When the map to traverse this terrain safely and easefully has been made available, our relationships become safe and easeful. We learn to truly connect, be seen, and see others. We can allow our partner to be who they truly are and become a true support for them in becoming more of who they want to be. We also are receiving the support we desire to step more and more into our own self-expression, where we become a sovereign being. There is a deep stillness in that relationship, one that only comes from fully trusting each other; trusting that the other person will not go away, will not judge, will not overpower, will not project, will not fight; a stillness that is the delicious savoring of experiencing true connection – connection as a phenomenon that just is, that is all the time but that we hardly ever tap into because we are so busy managing, covering, and hustling to get our unmet needs met.

When this energy is not properly activated, you tend to be in the throes of pulling and pushing; the old and tiring game of either needing and wanting someone who doesn't want us or to be the one feeling inundated, feeling suffocated, feeling like going away is the best way to go. Once you understand the integrate needs and wounds of your own shadow aspects pertaining to this archetype, nothing in the realm of relationships will remain a headache-producing mystery. It will actually become logical to you. And once you get the logic of something, it is so easy to solve. So easy, I promise you.

The deep understanding and resolving of the wound within the Lover archetype construct allow us to resolve the unresolvable.

Nathalie, a client who participated in an immersion designed to integrate the shadow aspects of the connection archetype shared with me that her way of relating to men had completely changed. Within a few weeks of the integrations, Nathalie completely shed any and all needs to impress a man, whereas before the immersion, impressing men, whether that be a brother, her father, an ex-husband, a future boyfriend, a lover, was a compulsion she was not even aware of.

Nathalie was constantly feeling that she had to prove her worthiness, be cool and independent and really desirable, and it was constant work. And all of that got completely wiped out from her way of being, without having to make any conscious effort at all. It just no longer occurred to her that she needed to impress a man. Instead, she shared she was now actually seeing men. She wanted to find out who they were; she wanted to connect with them where they are at and from a place of where she is at – no games, not frills, not pretense, just a genuine and transparent desire to see men for who they are. She started dating and felt completely free to be herself, enjoying the process.

The Archetype of Thriving, Also Known as the Mother and Father Archetypes

This archetype relates to the archetype of connection in a direct, almost logical way. The wound of the feminine version in the Lover archetype schema is created by the absence or intrusion by the father. Therefore, when integrating the Father archetype shadows, much of that stress that contributes to the wounding that takes place within the feminine Lover archetype can be alleviated.

One of the dynamics that contribute to dull and not-so-enjoyable relationships is when you look for fathering or mothering in your intimate partners or when you project your Father/Mother wounds onto your partner. It takes the sexual attraction out almost immediately. And yet, no one has any idea what happened and why, since maybe the sexual attraction was one of the predominant drivers of the relationship in the first place.

Remember the shadow of the feminine, child version of the Lover archetype is that of Daddy's Little Girl who never got the daddy she actually needed. He either violated her to some degree physically, sexually, or emotionally, or he abandoned her to varying degrees, anywhere from being completely absent to simply living in the household but being emotionally unresponsive. And out of that wound arises the other shadow aspect which is traditionally called the "Seductress" – I prefer to call her the hustler. She hustles to get some kind of male figure to pay attention to the either violated or abandoned aspect; she tries to either seduce the father with cuteness, tears, tantrums, or anything else for that matter to bring him back. Or, if he is the type invading the little girl's space, she helps her become invisible, shy, polite to no end, et cetera.

To come back to the Father and Mother archetype, you can start to see how they interrelate and how we unconsciously draw on the energy of a totally different archetype to make us feel better. However, as you can imagine, bringing Father and Mother energies into intimate relationships really can take the fun out of it. It is after all a totally different energy and is best left where it belongs, to fathering and mothering. In intimate relationships, we want to experience the true essence of connection and not have to father or mother someone else.

The opposite is quite true as well in that the part that is trying to cope with the wound that took place within the Father/Mother archetype schema is also trying to hustle and bring in someone to make up for the lack of fathering and mothering. That aspect often wanders off and tries, and often succeeds temporarily, to employ the shadow aspect of the Lover archetype. Again, not a good idea, as it does take out the fun from intimate relationships.

When you integrate the energies of the archetype of thriving (Mother/Father), you bring stability into your life; you bring a sense of belonging and nurturance into your life; your professional and/or financial life becomes more sturdy and supports you more. You simply start to feel more well-rounded, relaxed, like you belong here (wherever that is), and you have a deeper sense of general wellness. Having these qualities activated makes it that much easier to enter the delicate realm of intimate relationships.

When you are not looking for your intimate relationship to take care of your basic nurturing, your basic success in life, your basic stability, you can be much more in tune with the delicate dance that the true love relationship requires.

The Archetype of Self-Expression, Also Known as the Amazon and Warrior Archetypes

What does this energy have to do with creating and maintaining healthy, uplifting intimate relationships that allow each person to live in their full authenticity?

Everything.

For starters, as you may remember, the Amazon/Warrior energies are the ones who are responsible for you either having lousy, inexistent, mediocre, or fabulous boundaries. In order to thrive in any relationship, you need to know what your boundaries are and what the boundaries of the other person are, and you need to be willing to respect both. And you need to be willing to pay attention, be alert and attuned to adjust them on a daily basis because guess what? When you are allowed to have boundaries and the other person respects them, they actually change. We often have a need to assert boundaries that are extra safe, that give us extra space, until we learn that the other person deems that as okay and that the other person will abide by them. When you feel that respect and safety, it often allows you to shift your boundaries, as healing does take place when you are seen, respected, and supported in what you truly need.

Boundaries create clarity of who you are, what you need, what you stand for and so forth, and are not hard lines, walls or devices to create separation or threats.

Boundaries are not the only way in which the Amazon/Warrior energies play a major role in relationships. As you may recall, all the wounds and attempts to cope with them within the Amazon/Warrior schema are related to anger. And anger, as natural and inherent to being human it is, is the number one destructive force of connection. When anger is not dealt with in a life-giving manner, it will undermine at first and ultimately destroy the connection you most long for.

The art of owning and feeling anger and finding new ways of resolving it that do not involve suppressing anger or acting out on anger is the way to go. And that information on how you can best do that lies within the map of your inner Amazon/Warrior terrain. I can give you tips, ideas, and suggestions, but ultimately, each person has their own inner terrain; once you have been successful at doing the delicate and demanding work of integrating these energies, the map to the terrain will reveal the roads, the paths, and even the landscape will change. It will change from a dangerous, possibly mine-filled area, to a place of great clarity, direction, and purpose.

Acting on anger and also acting on unconscious anger destroys the connection you most want. There is no way around that, and unless and until you find a way to deactivate the anger that is stored way below the surface, you will inadvertently push the people you most care about away.

You may think to yourself that you are in touch with your anger, that you do not suppress it. I guarantee you that there is more. There is much, much more. When you recall the Collective Unconscious that we are all a part of you can just imagine the amount of anger there is between the sexes. Men and women have played a hard game, or shall we say they have been at war for a really long time, a war that has played out underground and also one that has played out in open battles. It is not a terrain to ignore or to turn your back to. It is vital; it is hard and quite frankly nasty work at times, and it must be done for us to create a new culture where connecting deeply with one another becomes the norm.

And when you think of wanting and desiring all of your relationships to be an expression of unconditional love, you can automatically see that you need really good boundaries.

The Archetype of Self Worth, Inner Knowing, and Intuition, Also Known as the Wise Woman and the Magician Archetypes

You may have noticed that I always mention this archetype last. It also is the one I work with last when I assist someone in integrating these energies. She, the Wise Woman, governs the entire landscape of them all. She is mysterious; she cannot be messed with; she keeps the overview and always has the last word.

Let's let her have her last word.

Without wisdom, without your own inner GPS intact, you are screwed. All the other archetypal energies are great and helpful, but without you actually knowing who you are and what is good for you, all of this is worth nothing. You need to unlock you own inner terrains and activate the maps, not someone else's. And there is nothing more powerful and that gives you immediate access than the Wise Woman/Magician energies.

They are rather simple and straightforward and also are the most complex and individually different when it comes to integrating them. They do not have the complicated ways of interaction with one another like, let's say, the Lover and the Mother/Father archetypes. They are kind of standing on their own, somewhat detached from the others.

The way I experience this energy in how it informs and directs intimate relationships is that when this energy is available, you know much faster what is true for you, what is not, what you need, what you don't. It gives you clarity about what you need and want from a deep place. And in order to have any good relationship, the one with yourself as well as the ones with others, you need to always know what you need and want in that moment of time, or else, you abdicate, you project, you deny and ultimately hold the other person responsible, or rather, blame them.

The Wise Woman/Magician archetype also is the one who holds the key to your sense of worthiness and your self-confidence. It is almost like a switch. Whenever I have assisted someone with integrating this energy, their sense of self-worth went way up, almost immediately. And I have not seen it come back down; it is kind of like a permanent switch. Having self-confidence and a sense of self-worth, I would say, is a key ingredient for a healthy relationship.

One interesting discovery I made is that a client of mine was able to uncover a deeply buried choice to have a physical disease that rendered her exhausted all the time within the complexities of the Wise Woman archetype. However, that was not yet giving her access to resolve the issue. That just opened the door for her to find the issue, which was buried within the complexities of the Connection archetype. There, she discovered that she had been so frightened to be abandoned that she created a disease that would always ensure at least someone would have to take care of her and stand by her – in other words, not abandon her. Once she was able to resolve the abandonment trauma within the Connection archetype construct, she then was also able to let go of the physiological manifestation.

It is important to evaluate if the way we have always been doing something might be based on outdated information, concepts, and beliefs. Much is changing in how humans do life on planet earth. And certainly, changing how we do relationships is way overdue. Unless of course, you think it is all dandy – in which case I am wondering why you are still reading this book.

In the US, there is a divorce rate of about fifty percent and are lots of different studies about the unhappiness of the fifty percent who remain married – altogether not a good indicator that we got this figured out.

As you go inside of yourself and you heal and integrate these shadow aspects of yourself, you change the Collective Unconscious. Each time someone dives in to re-engineer even a small aspect of it, it has a huge ripple effect on the whole. And eventually, we do stand the chance of re-formatting the Collective Unconscious. Every time something becomes conscious and forms a new way of being, every other human being on this planet gets a software update.

The Greek mythology is based on the archetypal energies, and it was firmly believed (and still is) that the mortal human beings are not able to live in the experience of the actual archetypal power. They can only get tangled up in the painful experience of the shadow aspects of each archetype. Therefore, this is called "tragedy." When we live out our shadow versions of the archetypal energies, we are bound to enact a tragedy, one that looks utterly personal and unique; however, when you take a closer look, you will see that each and every one of them is an enactment of the specific shadows and the combinations thereof. Which has been repeated by others before you, maybe a million times already?

Are you ready to eliminate tragedy from your life?

It requires courage – any journey out of the known into the unknown requires courage. That is true. Can it be done? Absolutely. Is the information provided to you in this book making it way accessible to you? Certainly.

Are you going to utilize it?

What would it take for you to make this choice to move out of tragedy?

What would you need to know, or be certain of, to make that choice?

What are your criteria for making such choices?

I recommend you journal about this question: What are your criteria for making a choice on setting out to change something or not, and what is it that you need to know about the approach so you can fully say yes to it?

Our relationships dominate the quality of our lives and also that of our neighborhoods, communities, and countries. They literally are the foundation of world peace.

For that reason, I invite you to take the courageous step and imagine right now what it truly could look like when all of your relationships are supportive and enjoyable and how that would affect world peace.

Relationships are the most paradoxical matter. They bring us so much joy and strength, and at the same time, when they go south, they can be the worst thing ever, and it is normal to write the importance of relationship off. We all do it. We tell ourselves that we are better off alone, as it causes much less trouble because diving into these deeply buried hurts and festering wounds is just not the commonly shared definition of fun.

Most of the relationship patterns we have inherited from generations ago are toxic in nature and lead to despair, frustration, confusion, violence, and most of all, loneliness.

I think you can look at doing this highly personal work as a means of contributing significantly to world peace.

Unsuccessful relationships also create other ways of hurting, such as lowering our immune system, lowering success rates in career and financial matters, bringing about anxiety and depression, sleep and/or weight issues, and so on.

On the other hand, when your relationships are well and sturdy, you can experience more self-confidence, a sense of worthiness, higher self-esteem, and just a general sense of wellbeing.

I delight when I see people who are in healthy relationships with one another; it is like they emit a sense of stability and happiness for everyone around. And when I hear of or see unhappy relationships, it truly hurts. We can all feel that hurt; we all know it, and we all had enough of it.

Will you join me in contributing to the new world we all create, the sense of deep belonging and connecting? A world, where we embrace and accept one another and ourselves, including our emotional needs? One where we are proficient in finding creative and effective ways of finding win-win solutions so everyone can be included and thriving?

I dream of a world where women can bask in their delicious, scrumptious, nurturing feminine nature while making huge contributions to this beautiful world.

I dream of a world where we embrace our own and each other's emotion as a beautiful expression of the divine beings that we are, a world where we are able to experience the beauty and depth of emotion so we can create meaningful and fulfilling connection with each another.

I dream that we cultivate a new way of living where the quality of relationships is of core value to everyone.

I dream that every woman is in a partnership that supports her and uplifts her so she can be her best and shine. The Dalai Lama allegedly said, "The world will be saved by the western woman." If that is so, then I think the western woman will stand a much better chance if she is with her beloved.

Chapter 13

To Change Your Life, You Need to Change Your Priorities

"To change your life, you need to change your priorities."
— Mark Twain

I have covered a lot of ground. In fact, we dug deep underground. How has this ride been thus far for you?

Are you utterly confused and more lost than ever, or have the doors to major insights and possible transformations opened up for you?

I first talked about how the modern human being relates to his own and other people's emotions – how there is a constant need to push and judge emotions rather than embracing and accepting them and what damage that causes in your formative years of zero to eight years old that will haunt you for the rest of your life, unless of course you choose to change that.

I talked about what happens in human children between ages zero to eight when emotions that are elicited in what seems like common day-to-day events are not fully experienced and integrated.

I talked about how wild it really is that once we have reached age eight most of us had to toss so many aspects of ourselves into our subconscious domain, such that we hardly know anymore who we actually are. And when these parts are not gently and lovingly retrieved, it causes a ruckus in your adult life; one particular ruckus can look like the relationship from hell.

It is safe to say that when these aspects of yourself that were not welcomed between age zero and eight are not available to you, it is hard, or let's be honest, it is not possible for you to live a life of full potential. Your potential is hidden far under the ledges, and you don't even know it is there.

I then went further and talked about the archetypes that make up the divine feminine and divine masculine energies and how when there is any form of emotional trauma, as in not having been able to fully integrate any and all emotional experiences, the archetypal energies too are not integrated and are not available to you. Not only that, they now show up in their shadow aspects, which, as we discussed, can be extremely and annoyingly destructive in building an awesome relationship.

In addition to that, I talked about how we are innately enmeshed with the Collective Unconscious. And how the information pool in the Collective Unconscious is a mere assemblage of dysfunctional relationship patterns, constructed by the archetypal shadow energies – a totally predetermined story of failure, loss, pain, and confusion. If you are the exception or you know one, congratulations.

I then went into detail of how the many archetypal energies and their shadow manifestations look in real life, in particular in relationships. I talked about the eight key archetypes – the four masculine ones and the four feminine ones. I talked about the child and the adult version of each. In total, I touched on thirty-two shadow aspects.

The Lover, or Connection archetype, holds the code for how we as humans can lead deeply connective lives. It holds the sacred map of how the feminine is designed to take the masculine into an inward journey to discover his own inner mystery. She opens the world of feeling and connecting to him, gifts that she as the feminine is endowed with by nature. It is a journey that requires great trust, gentleness, and calmness, a journey that when completed successfully leaves the masculine with a completely new perception of life — one where he can feel the moon whisper sweet nothings in his ears, one where he can relate to the tremendous effort migrating birds put forth every single day of their lives, one where he can appreciate the true flavor of a fresh raspberry.

The reward for the feminine is the deep, connected safety of belonging and being protected and provided for by the masculine.

Then we dove into the gifts that the Mother and Father archetypes hold for you, also referred to in this book as the archetypes of Thriving and Sustenance. When the ideal father and mother parent you, much of these energies integrate automatically. But then who does? Here you get your second chance of getting awesome parents when you integrate the Father and Mother archetype shadows (two child versions of the feminine, two child versions of the masculine, two adult versions of the feminine and two adult versions of the masculine — that makes eight out of the thirty-two total).

The way I like to describe this power pack of energies is the tomato plant. A tomato plant naturally grows as a vine and, if not supported, creeps along the ground. As a result, she may not get much sunlight, as other plants might tower over her; also, her precious fruit easily becomes food for slugs and all kinds of creatures coming around. The tomato would be the nurturing quality of the Mother energy; she gives sustenance. Without a tomato cage, her thriving is not guaranteed, and if she does make it, her yield will be significantly lower than that of the tomato plant that has a cage to grab onto and grow up on. When a good sturdy cage, the Father energy, is available, the Mother energy can thrive too. What it all comes down to is that the Father energy, who provides grounding, stability, and structure, is key to our thriving. When that masculine energy is available and activated, he ensures that the yield of all of our efforts is ample. He literally creates structures and systems for money to flow into life, to get it organized and optimized. I have heard from clients that it literally changes how they went about earning money; they moved from a fickle, unpredictable flow, to a sturdy flow they could rely on. And naturally, the nurturance, the warmth, softness, and kindness of the Mother energy that we all could tolerate some more of needs to be in a safe and sturdy container. If her container is not made sturdy by the Father energy, her ability to nurture and sustain is greatly impaired.

Isn't that such a mirror of what we so often see in families? An exhausted, possibly single mother, who is constantly on edge. She no longer has access to the inherent beauty of her own nurturance and snaps, stresses, is driven by anxiety and, much to her dismay, is not able to give her children the emotional support they need. And thus, the cycle beings all over again.

That is why I think that the best support a man can give to his young children is to take excellent care of their mother. Love her well, provide for her, make her comfortable and safe, and she will be the best mom there is.

Then we entered the wild territory of the Warrior and Amazon energies; I like to call them the archetype of Self-Expression. Truly, that energy has much wildness embedded in it and, hence, is massively suppressed by most. Yes, those two hold so much of the key to our ability to get what you want, including the right kind of mate, the right kind of relationship. With their energy activated, you have excellent boundaries, the kind of boundaries that allow for true connection, collaboration based on mutual respect. When something goes wrong with the integration of those energies at a young age, the way it looks like later is that you are either a half-comatose doormat or you are a raging nut case or somewhere in between, never quite comfortable with expressing who you really are, expressing your most vulnerable emotional needs, your most extravagant dreams and aspirations.

You absolutely need to find a way to integrate these energies of the Warrior and Amazon if you want to live a life of personal and professional fulfillment. This is the energy that allows you to even know what your preferences are to begin with. Many of us don't know what our needs, especially our emotional needs, are. This is also the energy that allows you to communicate your needs, wants, and dreams in a way that elicits support and collaboration from others. The archetype of full Self-Expression is something so many people strive and long for, yet no one wants to deal with the suppressed anger that is holding the energy locked.

And that is where it gets a little wild. When you allow the energies as they are intertwined with the sometime gruesome energy fed right from the Collective Unconscious, it can get a little intense. This is an integration, by the way, that I do not recommend you do on your own. You are either going to shortcut it – and thus shove things under the rug again (and each time it goes under, it gets uglier) – or you may not be able to really access it.

The war between women and men has been real and longstanding. The Amazon and Warrior archetypes hand us a key on a golden platter to unlock ourselves from that futile battle for good. Why not?

And then least but not last, we kissed the archetypal energies from afar, the Wise Woman and the Magician; I call them the energies of Inner Knowing. Obviously, we each have a unique life story, unique dreams and hopes, and our futures will also be uniquely different. In order to hone in on what exactly you really want (versus what you might think you want given our conditioning and expectations laid on us) and what turns to take and when and with whom, it would be good to have a good serving of inner knowing. It helps you to stay on course, not get sidetracked, be efficient with your time and resources, and get to your destination much faster.

It has been my great honor to share all of this information with you and to have lived a life that allowed me to gather all of this experience.

It is my deepest heart's wish that it benefits you greatly and that it will allow you to create the most loving, fulfilling, happy relationship you could ever imagine.

My wish for you is that you live a full and fulfilling life with your beloved on your side, a life where you get to be and express everything you are and do it in the company of people you not only love deeply but whom you really like.

My wish for you is that you find your beloved with whom you can enjoy life and who is on your side when the going gets rough because life is so much easier when shared.

My wish for everyone is that we all find a way of living together in harmony and happiness where we can assist one another in becoming more of who we are.

My wish is that you fall in love with your beloved and learn about the depths of your vulnerability, your femininity, your masculinity in a way that fills you with tremendous elation and a sense of invincibility, a feeling that you can do anything you want to do in this world and then do it together.

My wish for you is that you realized, reading this book, that the reins of your destiny are in your hands and that you can create and shape it as much as you are willing to dive deep and do the inner work that is required. It can be done, and you sure can do it.

My wish for you is that you allow yourself to find out that your own inner landscape is the most fascinating of all places and that if you dive in, you can indeed change your future.

My hope is that I have inspired you to take action and go for it. After all, is there anything more important than finally finding your beloved?

My commitment is to help repair and restore the sacred web that connects all of humanity.

The End

Acknowledgments

Thank you to all the people who so generously supported me in writing this book. And a very special thank you to:

- Dr. Hector Garcia for always having my back.
- Graciela Hernandez for being beyond amazing.
- Tina Wells for sending me the best friends ever.
- Röskva, Marshmallow-M&M-Sunny-Happy-Feet Maxi-chick & the gang, Luna, Bijou and Pantherina for your unconditional love, loyalty and protection.
- Marta Malinowska for recognizing my work and diving in deep.
- Nancy Allen and Monique Catoggio for always being there for me.
- Magda Strojna for being the force of nature that you are.
- Jen Vera for always supporting me.
- Ruth Jahn for your lovely Glitzerkugeln infusions.
- Tatiana Pletosu and Jane Phillips for keeping everything going.
- Albert Pellissier for believing in me.
- Thank you to Angela Lauria and The Author Incubator's team for helping me bring this book to print.

Thank You

Thank you so much for taking the time to read this book. I hope you enjoyed it and are ready to take your journey of finding your beloved to the next level.

If this has given you hope that finding your beloved is not just a possibility, but a probability, and you are inspired to take action, I would like to offer you a gift.

I created a free training so you can get started on finding your beloved right away. Please click here to access the training: https://rosinekushnick.com/freetraining/.

Or email me at rosine@rosinekushnick.com so I can send it to you, or visit my website at https://rosinekushnick.com.

Lots of love to you, and see you soon.

About the Author

Rosine Kushnick grew up on a small farm in Switzerland. She moved to New York City to attend New York University, and received a master's of fine art from State University of New York. She lives on a small farm in the Catskill Mountains of upstate New York, in close relationship with nature and all things.

All her life, she has been drawn to understanding the mystery of life, which has led her to practice meditation and to study various healing methods and approaches.

In 2008, her ability to speak was reduced to a whisper. Doctors predicted she would never be able to speak again. This experience taught her both about the invaluable gifts of speaking and deep listening. She was determined to find an alternative to what the doctors envisioned for her.

This healing quest led to meeting, studying, and learning from many great masters on a broad range of healing modalities and the subsequent training and certifications. Rosine reclaimed her voice, in more than one way.

Rosine now assists women to find their beloved through her uniquely designed programs and workshops.

Rosine draws on a wide range of knowledge, including the Completion Process, conceived and taught by Teal Swan, Soul Realignment by Andrea Adler, Innergetics by Dr. Hector Garcia, Matrix Energetics and Holo-Synchronous Energetic Technology Systems by Richard Bartlett, Herbalism, Chinese Medicine and Homeopathy, and she is also a Reiki Master. Rosine constantly adds new (and ancient!) modalities to her practice.